The Third World
and the
Soviet Union

The Third World and the Soviet Union

edited by

Zaki Laïdi

translated from the French by
A.M. Berrett

Zed Books Ltd
London and New Jersey

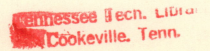

The Third World and the Soviet Union was first published in
1984 in French as *L'URSS vue du Tiers Monde* by Editions
Karthala, 22-24, boulevard Arago, 75013 Paris.

First published in English in 1988 by:

In India
Popular Prakashan, PVT Ltd., 35-C Pandit Madan Mohan
Malaviya Marg, Popular Press Building., Opp. 'Roche'
Tardeo, Bombay 400034, India.

In the rest of the world
Zed Books Ltd., 57 Caledonian Road, London N1 9BU, UK
and 171First Avenue, Atlantic Highlands, New Jersey 07716,
USA.

Cover design by Andrew Corbett
Typeset by EMS Photosetters, Rochford, Essex
Printed in the UK at The Bath Press, Avon.

British Library Cataloguing in Publication Data
The Third World and the Soviet Union.
  1. Developing countries——Foreign relations
  ——Soviet Union. 2. Soviet Union——Foreign
  relations——Developing countries.   3. Soviet
  Union——Foreign relations——1975-
  I. Laïdi, Zaki   II. L'URSS vue du Tiers
  Monde. *English*
  327.470172'4   D888.S65
  ISBN 0-86232-730-X
  ISBN 0-86232-731-8 Pbk

Contents

The Contributors

Françoise Cayrac-Blanchard. Researcher at the Centre d'Études et de Recherches Internationales. (FNSP) Author of 'Le Parti Communiste Indonésien'.

Georges Boudarel. Lecturer at the University of Paris. Author of *La Bureaucratie au Vietnam*.

Jean Copans. Lecturer at the École des Hautes Études en Sciences Sociales. Author of *Les Marabouts de l'Arachide*.

Zaki Laïdi. Researcher at the Centre d'Études et de Recherches Internationales. (CNRS)

Antonio Carlos Peixoto. Researcher at the Institute of International Relations, in Rio de Janeiro.

Elizabeth Picard. Researcher at the Centre d'Études et de Recherches Internationales. (FNSP)

Semih Vaner. Researcher at the Centre d'Études et de Recherches Internationales. (FNSP)

Max Zins. Researcher at the Centre d'Études et de Recherches Internationales. (CNRS)

Preface

Jean Leca

The 'external' image is part of the 'internal' image. Seeing beyond frontiers is a manner of seeing within them. In psychological terms, seeing, or refusing to see, the other, is a manner of seeing oneself. Knowing which image is the truly decisive one is a secondary problem, the answer to which will vary from case to case. The essential point is that the two processes of the social construction of reality cannot be separated. Even if there exist numerous (but not an infinite number of) forms of articulation between the two images, the logics of their construction do not operate in isolation from one another. Whence the interest of the contributions assembled in this book which generally avoid separating the image of the USSR produced by the various groups or governments in the Third World from the representations of the workings of the internal social and political system.

In truth, the problem is decidedly more complicated in so far as the combinations of images bring together not two poles (the internal one and its conflicts, and the external one, i.e. the USSR) but three, since the second external pole must be added to it, i.e. the West, the experience of which is combined systematically with the internal experiences of Third World societies. Again, to be complete, a fourth pole should really be added, that of the nearest 'exterior' in the region (for example Ethiopia for Somalia, Iran for Iraq). One single combination is thus not conceivable, but that does not mean that an effort should not be made to reduce it all to some sort of order.

A systematic enquiry ought to follow two paths: examination of how the image is produced, and examination of the image as a finished product.

The *production* of the image involves four distinct processes:

(1) Promotion, assured by the USSR itself by the message flows directly addressed to each country treated separately. The messages are directed at governments, but others are also aimed at society through exhibitions organized by Soviet Cultural Centres, invitations to various strategic groups, positions adopted on certain questions that are vital for the public opinion of a country, even the names and ethnic group of the representatives of the Soviet government or Soviet organizations. A whole marketing effort is systematically carried out virtually on a permanent basis aimed at sectors of varying importance: the intellectuals are often a special target when, for example, they come to pursue technical courses in a Soviet university to which will surely be added courses on official 'scientific' philosophy and ideology. Assessing the effectiveness of such promotion is not easy:

overestimating it leads to one getting caught up in the obsession with conspiracy which attributes superhuman virtues to Soviet propaganda. Underestimating it is scarcely wiser: advertising a brand does not guarantee that the target-public is going to rush out to sing its virtues, but nor does it guarantee the opposite. Political scientists, however, less fortunate than the advertisers of a brand of soap or the communication experts working on the televisual image of a democratic leader, lack the means to carry out surveys among students at the Patrice Lumumba University, the military in Benin, bureaucrats and tribes in South Yemen or militants in the Ethiopian party. That is probably why the contributors to this book pay little attention to the problem. It is an impossible task, for an uncertain result, and they are right not to pursue it.

(2) Information is also produced by other media which are not controlled by the USSR, in particular the main national or foreign media in the particular country. A study of newspapers can be useful for identifying the image of the USSR that those who control the media *want* to promote; the messages of the various secular movements (trade unions, professional associations or 'peace movements') or religious movements (Muslim or Christian sermons, churches, religious associations) equally merit study. As for assessing the effectiveness of these production lines, it is just as tricky, but it gives information about the attitudes of opinion leaders (or makers), even if there are grounds for scepticism about the notion of public opinion or its importance in some Third World societies.[1] Although they did not conduct any systematic study of it, our authors did not overlook this aspect of the problem.

(3) The third mode of production of the image depends on the predispositions to situate the USSR on a cognitive map drawn up in order to satisfy the interests and feelings of a group. The formation of a fundamental universe fixing the principal poles of antagonism, structures the perceptions of friends and enemies and puts the USSR in one or the other camp. The USSR thus becomes not just a great state power and hence criticizable as such but a piece in an ideological whole, whether as an exemplary model or as the first country to have put into effect a system of understanding the world, of acting on that world and of legitimizing the means of that action. This ideological system can provide both a system of support for state powers and a way of challenging them. On this interplay Jean Copans' chapter provides a provocative analysis; Zaki Laïdi's introduction places it within a general problematic which opens up many avenues of research and gives plenty of food for thought.

(4) Finally, the strategic experience of political elites (of governments and oppositions) also contributes to producing an image. This process is not similar to the previous one in the sense that it has less to do with internalized ideology and more to do with a conscious and instrumental rationality. The USSR is not only an ideological model, it is also a great power (including a military power) whose image will depend on the role that it plays (or may play) in North–South or South–South relations. Depending on the particular historical traditions, it will be considered as the heir of the Russian empire (as in the case of Turkey presented by Semih Vaner), the counterweight to the Chinese threat (for the Indian government, analysed by Max Zins, or Vietnam, analysed by Georges Boudarel), an immediate danger

through Vietnam for Thailand and Singapore, or a more remote one for the other countries of ASEAN (as Françoise Cayrac-Blanchard shows), an ally in the regional game and perhaps even a model of economic policy (and 'political economy') for the Ba'thist leaders of Iraq and Syria whose reservations, however, well brought out by Elizabeth Picard, relate both to what Syria sees as the excessively weak commitment of the USSR in the Palestinian conflict and to the shift in the internal Iraqi situation.

Of course these four processes of image production interfere with one another. The strategic experience is not purely instrumental, it can result from predispositions and contribute to 'post-dispositions' which become predispositions in a later stage. Those who broadcast information in the second process are also dependent on their predispositions and strategies (or those of their masters). Even the image promoted directly by the USSR depends not only on variations in Soviet policy but also on what the 'receiver' wants to accept. This image in turn helps in varying proportions to shape the information distributed by the media and to form predispositions and strategies.

The *finished product* is also a mix of factors. The image of the USSR is at once the image of a military, diplomatic and, to a lesser extent, economic 'power' influencing the international, and hence regional and sometimes national, game, and a perception of the bearer of an ideology, a credible incarnation of a movement which acts as a reference or repels. Whether one likes it or not, the image of the USSR cannot be separated from *an* image (not of course the sole one) of Marxism–Leninism. In a posthumous justification of the famous link between theory and practice and the primacy of social existence over consciousness, it is first of all as a Marxist state and only secondarily as the Russian empire (or 'heartland' in the geopolitics of Harold Mackinder) that the USSR is perceived, and the image of Marxism–Leninism can never be wholly separated from that of the 'fatherland of [actually existing] socialism'. Trotsky was perhaps right to speak of 'the revolution betrayed', but the country of the 'betrayal' of the revolution remains also the country of the historical Marxist revolution. The rest is, in a sense that is in no way pejorative, literature, pure speculation.

A paradox? The ideology of the post-bourgeois workers' revolution, of destroying the state and dispelling nationalism, is (through use of the Soviet Union as a reference point) instrumentalized, as Zaki Laïdi puts it; it serves as a legitimation for intellectual or military revolutions that are pre-bourgeois (since they sometimes serve to constitute a bourgeoisie, or rather a stratum of beneficiaries of economic goods obtained through control of political power), buttressing the state, proclaiming their nationalism out loud, crushing workers' revolts if need be.[3] Is all this something altogether novel and peculiar to the Third World? Marshal Stalin would doubtless smile into his moustache at the thought. History is so well acquainted with such tricks that they are often impudently attributed to the 'cunning of Reason'.

But a positive attitude to the USSR and, *a fortiori*, to Marxism, is the window-dressing for many widely different concrete arrangements, as varied as those covered by a negative approach and the proclamation of a competing ideology. In his remarkable essay on Black Africa, Jean Copans suggests linking adhesion to the

USSR to the existence of a network of national class alliances and a stage in the evolution of international capitalism. His thesis is clearly and strongly articulated, so that a paraphrase or summary would deprive it of much of its pith and it should be read very carefully. The following is a key passage:

> Recourse to the USSR is neither a last resort nor an illusion: it is a powerful instrument of learning about state power for social categories with no experience of the power of the bourgeois nation-state. Ideological coherence, the articulation between control of the masses, the administrative apparatus and police repression have, so it seems, a greater historical efficacy than the bourgeois tradition of the colonial apparatus.

The USSR would thus be playing the role of the Louis Napoleon Bonaparte of the *Eighteenth Brumaire*. Classes incapable of producing the hegemony and coercion that would make exploitation to their advantage possible are very glad to find a non-bourgeois political system to ensure a 'greater historical efficacy'. We should, however, note why this thesis fails as a general sociological thesis (and not as a historical explanation of specific cases, where we feel it is very strong): the phrase would be just as relevant if 'recourse to the USSR' was replaced by 'recourse to populist authoritarianism' in states (I am thinking in particular of Algeria[3] and Nasserite Egypt at some periods) where the reference to Marxism is very fragmentary and the image of the USSR of no great significance, despite the efforts of communist 'fellow-travellers'. And Elizabeth Picard's hypothesis, which is just as plausible in so far as Iraq is concerned, apparently contradicts Jean Copans: as the Ba'th became transformed into a *nomenklatura* of officials and made possible the growth of a new oil bourgeoisie, the reference to the USSR declined among the leaders (as they broke with the 'progressive forces', meaning the communists) and in the middle classes.

A more elementary explanation may be suggested. It is plausible that the Soviet reference is a particular case of a wider type: political elites, having no fixed place in the economic division of labour and dissatisfied with their place in the political division of labour, base their power on the 'primacy of the political' in a society where the classes of modern bourgeois society are not constituted and do not form a 'civil society', but where the rate of social mobilization is high. It is the revenge of the marginalized military, officials and militants, whom Marxism considers (along with the sub-proletariat) as secondary in the fundamental explanation of the modern political process. In this case the single (or dominant) party 'does not strictly speaking ensure the representation of the dominant strata on the political stage but fills the vacuum with respect to the state's claim to represent the nation'.[4] A positive image of the USSR is not necessarily an indispensable ingredient of this type of formula.

What can explain the presence of such an image in places where it does occur? Probably not the break with the capitalist world economy, which is a purely 'economistic' explanation ('Marxist–Leninist' South Yemen is as integrated as Ba'thist Iraq), any more than the nature of internal relations with the 'progressive forces', a purely 'political' explanation. (Excluding or driving out the communists, where they exist, whilst glorifying or respecting the Soviet model is not an achievement of which Iraq or Algeria alone had a monopoly in the mid-1960s. The first state to have supplied this model was . . . the USSR in the Stalinist years, which simply labelled these communists 'renegades'.) Strategic and cultural factors are important but probably less decisive than the appearance of a class struggle between a 'private' bourgeoisie owning the means of production or commercialization (and not satisfied with appropriating only their products) and a 'public' apparatus concerned with retaining control of the economic and political benefits associated with its place within the state. The distinction between public and private probably does not have any great significance in non-bourgeois societies, except when interpenetration between these two spheres, so barely autonomous in relation to one another, produces not an alliance but competition. The Soviet Union will then be used as a positive or negative reference point, according to the governments' attitude to the debate.

This hypothesis does not cover every possible case of this type. The reader will find several other configurations and other analytical schemas in this book. Their variety is precisely what makes it so interesting.

Jean LECA
Professor at the Institut d'Études Politiques de Paris

Notes

1. Why seek to reduce the phenomenon of public opinion to the existence of a bourgeois public sphere? The anecdote about some Somali (or Eritrean?) guerrillas suffering Ethiopian bombardments and certain they were being attacked by 'American Migs' is the (tragic) manifestation of a phenomenon of public opinion: only the (US) imperialists can attack anti-imperialist fighters. Migs are bombarding, so they must be American. This possibly apocryphal anecdote was told me by a *médecin sans frontière*. In 1939, the Polish communists (if there were any left) could have been attacked by German tanks coming from the eastern border . . .

2. John Kautsky, helped probably by his parentage ('the renegade Kautsky'), has pointed out that Third World revolutionaries, especially Marxist ones, are a variation of the 'modernizing elites' who take on the task of 'nation-building' in their societies. See J. H. Kautsky, *The Political Consequences of Modernization*, London, J. Wiley, 1972.

3. Curiously, the Algerian National Charter of 1976, a subtle mixture of Marxist and organicist language, says virtually the same thing as Copans: 'In the advanced countries socialism enjoys an enormous historical advantage, that of bourgeois society, its techniques, its know-how, its democratic traditions. In the backward countries, socialism has to create everything by itself including society, in its modern form, so as to make the Nation a free association of citizens.' The ideological assessment and the vision of the future are of course different and yet how can one avoid seeing in act and apology the process that Copans describes?

4. M. Camau, *Pouvoir et institutions au Maghreb*, Tunis, Cerès Productions, 1978, p. 13.

Introduction
What Use is the Soviet Union?

Zaki Laïdi

While analysis of the Soviet system and its articulation with the developed Western societies has generated a rich and extensive literature, the recent pattern of relations between the USSR and the countries of the Third World has not been the subject of any systematic reflection. The only major studies of the subject have mostly emanated from Western Sovietologists inclined to overestimate the Soviet factor and sometimes to reduce the expectations of developing countries to the mere satisfaction of limited diplomatic goals. Because of its failure to examine the mechanisms by which the Soviet Union is invoked as a model in developing societies, the Sovietological approach is forced to restrict the debate to the framework of inter-state relations. Even when it has tried to get beyond this level of analysis and take account of the perspective of developing societies, the conclusions that it reaches seem too often to be ideologically loaded and/or poorly buttressed methodologically. Thus, in his essay on the 'New Communist Third World', Peter Wiles is tempted to assess the authenticity of the Marxism-Leninism of the leaders of these states in the light of their professions of faith alone.[1] In fact, it is all rather as if the essays in 'tropical Sovietology' were limited to speculating on the possibility of transferring to the Third World the Soviet pattern imposed on Eastern Europe, with perhaps a few necessary adjustments to this transposition through often vague references to 'local conditions' or the 'nationalism of Third World leaders'.[2]

In stressing here the weaknesses of these 'Soviet-centred analyses' we are not seeking to replace them by an analysis that ignores the reality, the brutality even, of the international relations of forces. It is rather a matter of reversing the perspective, looking at things from the other end, and suggesting a framework for analysis that brings out the image of the USSR as seen from the Third World and identifies the function of this image in Third World states.

From the outset, this ambition runs up against many obstacles, not the least of which is the extreme variety of situations covered by the expression Third World. The social, political and diplomatic heterogeneity of the realities which we will touch on is probably impossible to exaggerate. Our discussion will, however, try to develop an analysis that links the internal socio-political dynamics of the developing countries and the configuration of diplomatic and strategic relationships into which their relations with the Soviet Union are inserted.

At the heart of our discussion we shall thus try to pose three series of questions.

The first, which seems to be historically the most important, concerns the connection between Marxism and the Soviet Union in the Third World. To what extent has Marxism in the Third World been thought of and diffused in reference to the USSR? Is the USSR perceived as an ideocratic power, purveying an ideology of universal significance, or simply as a strategic great power? In relation to what historical, geopolitical or cultural coordinates is the use of the Soviet Marxist reference facilitated or hampered? In order to answer this series of questions, we shall put forward the hypothesis that the connection between Marxism and the USSR was established at a precise historical moment (the stage of the national liberation of peoples), which greatly helped promote the assimilation of Marxism to Soviet (Leninist, and later Stalinist) Marxism and thus helped give the Soviet model a largely *instrumental* character in the developing countries.

From there, it will be possible to go on to discuss the features of Soviet reality reproduced in the developing societies. We will raise questions especially about the role of the state as the main focus for the use of the Soviet model, be it on the international stage, or when faced with civil society and the imperatives of economic and social development. We shall also have to reflect on the fragmented use of the Soviet world, its 'indigenization', its dissociation, in some situations, from Marxist ideology. In all these typical cases, the instrumentalization of the Soviet model can be analysed only in terms of the particular geopolitical conditions which shape the relations of a country or a group of countries with the USSR. The existence (or absence) of ideologies competing with Soviet Marxism, which might strengthen (or weaken) the fragmented use of the Soviet model are also relevant. In this connection, the Soviet model's role in the modern political culture of Third World societies seems absolutely essential. The capacity of a given political culture to imitate, appropriate or, on the contrary, reject the Soviet model poses a major problem. It conditions (just as much as arms deliveries and military advisers) the eventual establishment of this model in the Third World. That is why, lastly, we will pose the problem of the Soviet model in relation to its degree of 'internalization' in the political culture and make a few hypotheses on the possible formalization of the model as a *language of political discourse*, i.e. its emergence as a recurrent trait, as a 'legitimate problematic' (Bourdieu) within the contemporary political culture of a country or group of countries in the Third World. In this way, we can hope to go beyond the ideological simplifications maintained around the 'irreversibility' of the Soviet presence in the Third World.

Historical coordinates of the Soviet model

Apart from the special cases of Afghanistan, Iran and Turkey, where the contemporary representation of the USSR is based partly on a perception of Russia, relations between the USSR and the Third World usually rest on a very slight historical basis. But, from its very inception, the Bolshevik revolution sought to link up with the growing liberation movement of the colonized peoples of Africa and Asia. The historical context, theoretical considerations and contingent factors that facilitated this link-up are today too well known for us to go over them again here.

What it is important to analyse is the specific conditions in which the assimilation of Marxism to Soviet Marxism occurred in the Third World. For that, we need to ask about the historical meaning or meanings that the Marxist model assumed initially in the Third World, the social forces that carried it and the political sites within which it developed.

In what, at the beginning of the 20th century, constituted the Third World, Latin America occupied an altogether special place. On this sub-continent, where the struggle for national independence had broadly been completed by the end of the 19th century, the introduction of Marxism, its assimilation and then its appropriation were effected more in a context of social liberation and class struggle than of strictly national emancipation. Such has not been the case in other regions of the Third World where Marxism was initially perceived, thought and interpreted in relation to the colonial question. Faced with the Western powers, Marxism soon appeared as 'a method for denunciation, with a scientific basis . . . and a definite emotive value'.[3] It was widely used as an unchallengeable mode of access to universality against a colonial system organizing (to use Jean Leca's expression) 'the illegitimate specificity of the colonized'. Of course, at the dawn of the 20th century, Marxism could not alone claim a monopoly of access to universality. Reference to the French Revolution and its ideals offered the dual advantage of being assimilated by the transmitters of the message and perfectly intelligible to its intended receivers (the colonial government). But, it had the major disadvantage of being generally purveyed by the advocates of a compromise with the colonial government on the basis of assimilation, or even acculturation (such as Ferhat Abbas in Algeria) and of being difficult to understand for peoples for whom the assertion of otherness was the prime reflex of the struggle for emancipation. Marxism (or more precisely its vulgar form) partly overcame this contradiction (identity/universality) by turning against the West the weapons of positivist rationalism, while setting itself up as a 'system that was more consistent and critical towards the bourgeois West'.[4] Access to universality through Marxism thus fulfilled three mobilizing functions: it enhanced the legitimacy of the liberation struggle by opening it up; it placed it in a universal historical movement which was bound to speed up mobilization ('we are not alone') and help to overcome certain obstacles ('our victory is certain'); and it presented itself as a body of analysis making it possible to reconcile the demands of the nationalist struggle (and the risk of a withdrawal into a narrow identity) with the imperatives of modernity ('catching up with history', Abdallah Laroui was to say).[5] Finally, by conceptualizing a dialectical relationship between specificity and universality, Marxism appeared as the ideological method most suited to a new understanding of existing contradictions. Tribal, ethnic and religious cleavages deemed to be out-dated could be recast as the fundamental contradiction between the colonized/dominated and the colonizers/dominators. Marxism appeared as a *substratum* 'taking into account every form of oppression and arranging them in terms of one overriding opposition'.[5]

This is a vital dimension which will help us to better understand the role of Marxism as a system of representing social space. Thus, in one of the chapters of this book, Elizabeth Picard stresses the major contribution of the Kurds and

Christians, as ethnic–religious groups, to the formation of communist parties in Syria, Iraq and Lebanon. This seems all the more interesting to study because the social status of these minorities generally did not predispose them to refer to Marxist ideology.[7] The development of Marxism in the Third World around the anticolonial struggle (and not around the class struggle) reflects the plasticity of an ideology which is yet alleged to be deterministic and Eurocentric. Historically, it was the emergence of Soviet Russia as the first socialist state that *initially* favoured such an evolution. The nationalists in the Third World could then learn from this unparalleled historical experience the use of a theoretical tool in concrete circumstances. This capacity of the Bolsheviks to force their way through unfavourable 'objective conditions', thanks to a militarized organization and an unquenchable voluntarism, was not without its attractions to forces hostile to any compromise with the colonial government. This partial and perhaps provisional reconciliation of Eurocentric Marxism with nationalitarian ideology was in part the work of Lenin. It was continued by Stalin who elaborated, justified and popularized the idea of 'socialism in one country', in other words the strictly national appropriation of a messianic and universalist ideology.[8] As we shall see below, this historical connection was to be decisive for the identification of Marxism with Soviet Marxism and in the instrumental appropriation of the Soviet 'model'.

The initial perception of Soviet Russia was undeniably reinforced by its first anti-Western diplomatic initiatives, in the Middle East, for example (hostility to the Sykes–Picot agreements, support for Kemalist Turkey). It is, in this respect, particularly enlightening to reread the remarks made about the October revolution by Rashid Rida, the inspirer of the Muslim Brothers in Egypt. While clearly stating that this could not serve as a model for Muslims, he frankly recognized its merits as an anticolonialist and anticapitalist social and political movement.[9] The triumph of the Bolshevik revolution, which coincided moreover with the agitation of the Arab nationalist movement in the aftermath of the First World War, assisted the political radicalization of its fringe elements and the adoption in a number of cases (Messali Hadj's *Etoile Nord-africaine*) of Leninist structures. This nationalist radicalization, fuelled by the Bolshevik experience, was even more marked in Vietnam where the new Communist Party (CP) came rapidly to exercise a hegemony over the whole nationalist movement. But this convergence between Marxism and nationalism on the basis of a dual identification as both positivist and anticolonialist was historically neither linear nor uniform. As a general rule, the impregnation of the nationalist movement by Marxism remained narrowly circumscribed for reasons to do with both the political conditions of developing societies and the evolution of the USSR's international strategy. The only significant example of total appropriation and reinterpretation of Marxism in the Third World occurred in the 1920s in Latin America under the influence of Mariategui in circumstances that have more to do with social liberation than with national aspirations. But, as Michael Lowy clearly shows, even in that region, Marxism, initially creative, was to fall victim to the 'Stalinist freeze' imposed by the local communist parties from the 1930s onwards.[10]

In the other parts of the Third World the rigid strategy adopted by the Communist International after 1928 only helped to deepen the gap between the nationalist movement and the embryo local communist parties. In the Maghreb, for example, the Messalist movement distanced itself from the Communist Party when Thorez was advocating the 'fraternity of the races' in Algeria. In the Middle East, the relationship was more complex since it was built around the twin problems of independence and Arabism. But, while the first goal enabled the nationalists and communists to combine their efforts during the inter-war period, the second one was of a kind to fuel their disagreement. So, as the nationalist parties built up their own structure and succeeded in dispensing with the support of their former allies, they developed an anti-communist platform and laid claim to a monopoly over the national revolution and even over Arab socialism. The most sustained effort in this direction in the Middle East emanated from the Ba'th party, starting in the 1940s. The conditions in which this party developed in Syria and Iraq underline the ambivalence of the specific context in which the Soviet model was to be perceived and then used. To a considerable extent, the USSR's ordering of diplomatic priorities helped maintain, to a greater or lesser degree, suspicion of that country among the nationalists. The USSR's quick recognition of Israel was not without consequences on the historical development of its image in the Middle East. But, at the same time, the organizational practices of the communist parties, the anti-imperialist rhetoric, the idea of a state-led authoritarian modernization and the ethic of sacralizing secular projects all influenced an Arab nationalist movement led by populist strata purveying a project for national and social revolution. This ambivalence, which would be found in other regions of the Third World, was facilitated by the Stalinist thesis of socialism in one country. In some respects, this theory enlightened Third World countries as to the priority given by the USSR to the defence of its state interests. But in other respects, it paradoxically reinforced and justified expectations of what could be done alone, under difficult conditions – even without a communist party! It sustained the illusion that national revolution and social revolution were necessarily simultaneous processes. The impact of this dimension of Stalinist reality is amply demonstrated by its influence, especially in Black Africa, long after the death of Stalin and the 20th Congress of the CPSU.

Until 1945, however, the USSR's image remained vague both because of the limited scope of the nationalist movements and the incapacity of the USSR to make a real impact beyond its borders. This reality was perhaps reflected in Soviet–Turkish relations in the 1920s and 1930s. Turkey's hostility to the Western powers, the priority given to state-led economic development and the Kemalist government's quest for secular legitimacy ought to have facilitated the partial establishment of a Soviet-type model in the country. This hypothesis is far from gratuitous. One need only remember the efforts of the *kadro* group to extend to Kemalist Turkey Soviet practices of planned development.[11] Of course, many other factors, including the profound anti-Russian feeling of the Turkish population, were enough to counteract any reappropriation of the Soviet model. But what is worth stressing here is that the attractive power of the Soviet model is dependent on the diplomatic, military or economic options open to the Soviet Union at the particular time. Quite obviously, what the USSR can undertake in the Third World in the present decade could scarcely be envisaged half a century ago.

Following the Second World War, the worldwide spread and growing scale of the nationalist movement in the Third World coincided with the emergence of the

USSR as joint manager of the world order, even though strategic parity between the two superpowers would only be reached 30 years later. There ensued an undeniable heightening of the USSR's image. Nothing could better illustrate this than the Suez crisis. Just when the Krushchev report and the invasion of Hungary were further undermining the Soviet model in the West, the failure of the Anglo-French intervention in Egypt was raising Moscow's prestige in the Third World. By then, the USSR could no longer claim a monopoly of building socialism, because of the Chinese and Yugoslav experiences, but, thanks to the power of the means available to it, it did figure as the main proponent of 'actually existing' socialism in the world. In addition, the use made of the Maoist model by certain revolutionary groups was not altogether inconsistent with an appropriation of the Soviet model.[12] Thus, by endeavouring to valorize disjointedly or simultaneously the universality of its historical experience, the rapidity of its economic development or the effectiveness of its diplomacy, the USSR offers itself as a model in three crucial areas in the Third World: political legitimation, state-building, and finally, national self-assertion.

The instrumentalization of the Soviet model

The very concept of 'Soviet model' appears today, at least nominally, to be largely discredited. All the USSR's allies, not to mention the USSR itself, now deny the idea of a 'royal road' leading to socialism and opened up by the Soviet revolution in 1917. But, while they loudly and strongly proclaim the existence of national paths to socialism, they still continue to ridicule 'national socialisms'. Samora Machel liked to mock the blossoming of national socialisms in Africa: to talk of 'Mozambican socialism' would be as ridiculous as to postulate the existence of Algerian mathematics!

In the West, the concept of model has taken on a decidedly pejorative meaning. It is virtually used to mean the reproduction of 'actually existing socialism' perceived in terms of the hegemonic power of the USSR, its totalitarian system, and its failing economy. The Soviet model is then held up as a scarecrow intended to warn off any who might be tempted to follow it or have it imposed upon them.

Rather then than talking of a model, which evokes the idea of passive replication of Soviet reality, it would perhaps be more accurate to suggest the concept of a *Soviet reference point*. This could then be defined as the *process of replication of certain realities of the Soviet system under different historical conditions and for purposes that are not necessarily congruent, either with the meaning given them by the Soviets, or with the diplomatic or ideological objectives of the USSR*. From this definition two essential characteristics of the process can be deduced. The first concerns uses of the Soviet reference point which can, up to a certain point, be dissociated from the USSR. (The extreme case being that of a ruling party that is violently anti-Soviet but whose organization and functioning rests, for example, on democratic centralism.) The second, which flows largely from the first, relates to the very often fragmented manner in which the Soviet Union is used as a reference point. The reproduction of the discourse, organizational structures and modes of functioning of Soviet political systems and diplomatic behaviour is sometimes a *complete* reappropriation of all components of the original, sometimes a *fragmented* and partial reappropriation. Thus, through analysis of the representations of the world (discourse), their internal expression (organization and functioning of the political system) and external expression (diplomatic behaviour), it will be possible to locate the specific 'Soviet referents' adopted or rejected, before interpreting the meaning of these choices.

The Soviet Union as a reference point for political legitimation

Three central variables determine to what extent the Soviet Union is used as a reference point by Third World regimes seeking legitimation.

The first, which today appears to be the essential one, can be linked to the USSR's contribution to the political fortunes of the regimes in question. Generally speaking, the more decisive the USSR's contribution, the greater the chances of a complete appropriation of the Soviet Union as a reference point. Between the Castro revolution, whose triumph owed strictly nothing to the USSR, and the success of the MPLA in Angola, made possible thanks to Soviet–Cuban help, there are differences of kind with undeniable implications as to how these governments legitimize themselves internally. The Castro regime took more than 15 years to provide itself with a party structure based on the Soviet model. Conversely, in Angola as in Ethiopia, adoption of the Soviet Union as a reference point (through officially claimed adoption of Marxist–Leninist ideology) followed hard on Soviet–Cuban military intervention. The Soviets' repeated calls on the Ethiopian regime to endow itself with a properly constituted communist party is a good reflection of the partly 'suggested' character of this process. It might equally be thought that these countries' alignment on the most questionable positions of the USSR (Afghanistan, for example) is not totally unconnected with their military dependence on Moscow, especially when one compares the diplomatic behaviour of these states with that of such other 'Marxist–Leninist' African states such as the Congo or Benin.[13]

Yet, it is in terms of legitimation and not of mere vassalization that the use of the Soviet Union as a reference point is posed at this level. Once it turns to the USSR to secure power and maintain itself there, a regime finds itself constrained to define the bases of its legitimacy. It can then draw on a discourse, an organization of government and a diplomatic behaviour inspired by the USSR, not only for the instruments of its legitimation but also for the vehicles of its consolidation and external affirmation.

For liberation movements taking power following a struggle against colonialism alone, the legitimacy of Soviet support is usually unproblematic. But then it is generally among such governments that the way in which the Soviet Union is used as a reference point following independence is most fragmented (Algeria, Guinea-Bissau). It is limited to the appropriation of organizational methods 'tried and tested' during the struggle and to the 'anti-imperialist' (external self-assertion) and 'mobilizing' (maintaining the impetus for unity) elements of Soviet discourse. Conversely, in situations where Soviet support makes itself felt in a context of disputed legitimacy (internal rivalries and indecisive external pressure) and in which nationalist legitimation appears inadequate, the likelihood of a more complete appropriation of the Soviet Union as a reference point is greater (Afghanistan). Between these two extremes, the cases of Angola and Ethiopia (internal rivalries but undisputed external pressures) give us interesting examples of intermediate situations.

But, while this first variable seems important, it is not invariably decisive. The Cuban and Vietnamese regimes, which in no way owe their original legitimacy to the USSR, have today rejoined the 'socialist commonwealth'. On the other hand, for these two regimes, as for those in Angola, Ethiopia or Mozambique, the existence of strong external pressure partly explains the complete rather than fragmented way in which the Soviet Union is appropriated as a reference point. For these states, intensification of the external pressure produced almost mechanical effects on the modes of legitimation. At the diplomatic–strategic level, accentuation of external constraint impelled these states to seek a formalized politico–military guarantee, whose nature (treaty of friendship and cooperation, integration into the CMEA) varied with the scale of the threat and the willingness of the USSR to respond to it. In most cases, it also went hand in hand with the adoption of an international viewpoint coinciding more and more with that of the USSR. Judging the maintenance of an equal distance between the blocs neither possible nor desirable, these states come to see in non-alignment the prime expression of a refusal to side with the Western powers. This approach, interpreted in the West as the expression of a servile diplomatic alignment, is presented by these states as the manifestation of a natural alliance with the socialist states, preliminary to their ultimate integration into the world socialist system. The further removed from the USSR they are geographically, the more such an alliance seems useful to them because their geographical distance from the USSR shelters them from any possible 'fraternal interventions'. In fact, while Soviet aid undeniably creates for its beneficiaries 'duties' of allegiance directly proportional to the scale of the support granted, it is impossible to overlook, in these 'besieged states', the impact of seeing the challenges that they face at the regional level elevated to a global scale. Because these regimes confront adversaries enjoying the direct support of the Western countries (South Africa for Angola and Mozambique, the United States for Cuba), their receptiveness to Soviet theses about the polarization of issues around the East–West dimension is *a priori* all the greater. In addition, any weakening of the position of a USSR that is guaranteeing their survival is interpreted as a weakening of their own camp. This global reasoning in no way excludes the formulation of 'reservations' with regard to this or that aspect of Soviet behaviour. But, it inevitably structures the perception these states have of the USSR's place in the international system.

In these particular geopolitical conditions, their interest in an appropriation of the Soviet Union as a reference point goes beyond the diplomatic framework. In fact, starting from a 'war situation', the Soviet historical experience and discourse provide a precious ideological and technical arsenal to order contradictions and priorities or to justify oppressive behaviour and repressive practices. The apology for repression (re-education centres, security services) as a way of strengthening the state and socialism, the identification of the class enemy with the external enemy, and the fetishism of state power, characteristic of some African and Arab political

discourse today, appear to be largely inspired by the Stalinist ideological code.[14]
The explanation of every aspect of social, political or diplomatic reality in terms of
the 'external threat' then becomes a holistic principle, which undeniably facilitates
the use of the Soviet Union as the fundamental reference point.

But while diplomatic–strategic imperatives play no small role in determining to
what extent the Soviet Union is appropriated as a reference point, they are by no
means the sole factor. The process never takes place in a virgin political space.
Those purveying the Soviet Union as a reference point are forced to take their
bearings and adapt it to an already-existing culture, understood here in the sense of
a sharing by a population of a 'signifier-thing signified relationship, which means,
for example, that while disagreeing on what political action should consist of, two
actors nevertheless give the same meaning to the political . . . [and] express their
understanding of institutionalized power within the same frame of reference'.[15]

The more the use of the Soviet Union as a reference point has to be situated in
relation to an all-embracing political culture, the more its complete appropriation
appears as either difficult or useless. And, in this respect, the contrasting realities of
Latin America, the Arab world and Black Africa bear out our hypothesis. Despite
the fact that they belong to the developing world, the various geopolitical areas of
the Third World are at different historical moments. Thus, unlike Black Africa,
Latin America has a true national ideology. This historically derived differentiation
is fundamental. In Latin America, the national ideology has precisely produced a
specific political culture in which the values of patrimonialism or charisma, for
example, are so important that all social and political groups are obliged to refer to
them. Indeed, they constitute a hindrance to the penetration of Marxism, as
Antonio-Carlos Peixoto clearly shows in the last chapter of this book.
Furthermore, even in political groups claiming allegiance to Marxism, the
appropriation of Soviet Marxism is hindered, as we have seen, by a specific
historical tradition of assimilation of Marxism. In Black Africa, the dominant
ideology remains the nationalist ideology based on what Jean Copans calls in this
book 'maturation through external opposition'. Given the weakness of traditions
of revolutionary struggles, the persistence of forms of tribal loyalty, the fragility of
national feeling and the non-internalization of competing modern political
cultures, it seems that those ruling groups who derive from liberation movements
find it easier to reappropriate the Soviet Union as a reference point. They find in it
building blocks for a code of anti-imperialist legitimation, justifying the 'continuity
of tasks' following independence and hence their own continued presence in power,
at the same time as a way of producing a national ideology to mask the inevitable
construction of a system of domination. Between Latin America and Black Africa,
the Arab world occupies an intermediate position. The building of nation-states is
still relatively recent there, and Pan-Arab and Islamic ideologies strongly pervade
the political culture. The Pan-Arab ideology purveyed by Ba'thism and Nasserism
contributed greatly to providing a base for the legitimacy of regimes emerging in
most cases from *coups d'état* (Egypt, Syria, Iraq, Libya). But, since the 1967 Arab
defeat, the death of Nasser and the 1982 Israeli–Palestinian war, these sources of
legitimation have tended to dry up.

In Egypt, following the failure in 1961 of the merger with Syria, Nasser took stock of the limits of the legitimation of his rule through Pan-Arabism alone. He then embarked on the definition of a radicalized domestic policy, of which the National Action Charter was to be the cornerstone. Rejecting any form of Arab, national or Muslim socialism, the Charter claimed to be based on scientific socialism. In order to realize this new ideological project – notably through the reactivation of the single party – Nasser did not hesitate to release Egyptian communists from prison and make use of their talents. For the Egyptian regime, it was not a matter of forging new alliances, but of providing itself with an alternative mobilizing ideological project based notably on the fragmented appropriation of the Soviet Union as a reference point. It proved very difficult to give this project concrete shape: at its peak, in 1965, the ASU (Arab Socialist Union) never succeeded in mobilizing more than five million members, whereas the Muslim Brotherhood had over two million members . . . 20 years earlier. The comparison is all the more interesting as between 1948 and 1965 the Egyptian population had almost doubled.[16]

Since the relative failure of the Nasserite experience, the Arab regimes have thus been tempted to resort to the realm of political imagination to find forms of legitimation capable of mitigating or camouflaging the disappointments of Arab unity. Thus, in Libya, the announcement of the 'Third universal theory' and the birth of the *Jamahiriya* (the state of the masses), rejecting any structure based on parties, coincided with the first disappointments of Colonel Qadhafi about the rapid unification of the Arab nation. In Syria, the political failure of the Ba'thist regime led it to activate 'prepolitical forms of legitimacy' based notably on communal solidarity (*'assabiya*).[17] These forms of legitimation ruled out or invalidated the use by these regimes of the Soviet Union as a reference point, whatever the scale of their political relations with the USSR, especially since the dominant Islamic political culture, itself the bearer of a universalist and monistic project, identifies the USSR as an atheistic country.

Starting from certain Third World regimes' more or less extensive or complete use of the Soviet Union as a reference point, to legitimize their rule, there is a whole series of further relationships relating to *how* it is used. Let us hypothesize that the more complete the use of the Soviet Union as reference point, the more explicit will be the invocation of the USSR itself.

Whereas in Angola the leading role of the USSR in the building of socialism in the world is explicitly recognized, in Algeria on the other hand the progress of socialism is linked to the process of national liberation and not to the experience of the USSR. The 1976 Algerian National Charter, which declares that it is enriched by 'the contributions of the world socialist experience', nevertheless rejects any idea of 'Soviet centralism'. It considers socialism as 'the common heritage of humanity' and postulates that 'any revolution, if it is to be socialist, must first be national'.

The more complete and explicit it is, the more use of the Soviet Union as a reference point takes on a totalizing ideological content. The more fragmented and implicit it is, the more it appears as symbolic or instrumental.

Thus, in Cuba, the Soviet reference point is used in all its dimensions. It is different in Mexico where a very fragmented Soviet reference is used by a conservative government with the sole aim of blocking any rival political project. It stresses that, like the October revolution, the Mexican revolution is complete and that all those who dispute its achievements are necessarily part of a 'counter-revolutionary' process. On the same lines, the Zambian regime, which is profoundly anti-communist, suddenly declared itself Marxist–Leninist in 1982 so as to be better able to fight the labour movement accused of 'capitalist deviations'.

This indigenization of the use of the Soviet Union as a reference point in a perspective which no longer has any relationship to the contemporary USSR is even more widespread in countries interested in techniques of power deriving from the Soviet Union. Thus the one-party state in the most anti-communist country in Africa (the Ivory Coast) still today declares itself to be based on democratic centralism, inherited from the old alliance between the RDA and the French Communist Party. The Soviet reference, stripped of any legitimizing character, then takes on a purely instrumental content, intended usually to hasten the process of state-building.

The Soviet model and state-building
In most new states, the decisive stage of state-building is usually articulated around three objectives: to produce an ideology of state power capable of providing a new code of allegiance to the nation-state framework; to give an impetus to economic and social development aimed at 'catching up with history'; finally, to promote the establishment of new structures of rule adjusted to the interests of the social groups that are the direct beneficiaries of political independence.

As an instrument for breaking with segmented forms of allegiance and rapidly and effectively bringing to heel a recalcitrant civil society, the Soviet-derived statist model is certainly attractive. It provides an example, both historical and contemporary, of a country shot through with vast disparities, where the state has succeeded, in record time, in integrating civil society into a pre-established framework at the price of a voluntarism legitimized by the formula, state = masses. This model, based on standardized practices of organizing the political system (centralization, unification, hierarchization), has a much greater instrumental value than the functional Western model resting on the separation of powers, the diffusion of authority or the valorization of conflicting opinions. The single-party regime, charged with purveying a code of unanimity, appears as an instrument for legitimately disqualifying certain social groups, and that is so whatever the ideological system of reference adopted.

However, this political model, which had its hour of glory in the 1960s, is today partly discredited. Even if ruling political classes generally continue to lay claim to and defend it, some former single-party theoreticians (Lissouba in the Congo) and 'practicians' (Ben Bella in Algeria) are today revising their judgements. They blame such a system for both political authoritarianism and economic failures. If this sort of questioning were to spread, it would obviously have an impact on the political fortunes of the Soviet reference in the Third World.

The Soviet statist model, being an instrument of political control, also comes with a simplified set of instructions on how to use it for the reproduction of the logic of state power. In accordance with the Leninist theory it is enough to shift the actors around within the state to alter the course of history. Since the state has been taken over by the agents of a 'revolutionary' political project, it necessarily becomes 'revolutionary'. Yet this sort of political naiveté, fought by Rosa Luxemburg and described by her as the theory of 'the inverted capitalist state', has won many admirers in the Third World. In states that claim to be revolutionary, the post-colonial state is often only a pale reflection of the colonial state. Even in a country such as Ethiopia, which never experienced the colonial state, the 'socialist state' looks today very much like the heir of the Amharic state. The two mainstays of the imperial regime (the army and the administration) have come through the bloodiest phases of the revolution unscathed and the political–police technology imported from the USSR functions in perfect symbiosis with the centralizing straitjacket inherited from Menelik.[18] This statist logic, very briefly described, usually ends up in the reproduction of two salient features: the reduction and assimilation of social transformation to simple affirmation of a political will; and the more or less systematic marginalization of all rival forces likely to threaten the absolute monopoly of the state over public life. Thus agrarian reforms christened 'revolutions' will be launched by mere administrative fiat with great fanfare without prior political mobilization, alleging the urgency of the situation as an excuse. In actuality, these projects for radical change imposed from above enable the central authorities to maintain their control over the political process and to forestall, for example, the establishment of an autonomous peasant movement. The impact of these administrative revolutions is all the greater because they often borrow from Soviet discourse all its disparaging references to 'mass spontaneity' (justifying their regimentation), 'leftist illusions' (legitimizing the repression of student vanguards for example) or 'reactionary resistance movements' (usually foreshadowing the use of 'revolutionary violence'). At the same time the hypothetical 'New Man' will be endowed with all the virtues; rational, modern and standardized, his mentality transformed and cleared of 'survivals of the past'. The illusion of a 'radical break' is then trumpeted all the more because it often masks very limited social or economic changes. Thus deified, the 'Revolution' becomes something much too serious to be left in just anybody's hands. And the more resistance it encounters, the more it steps up its voluntarism, thus opening the Pandora's box of bureaucratic coercion, sometimes with the support of Soviet, East German or Cuban advisers.

Economically, the hegemony of the state usually results from the political eclipse of the liberal bourgeoisie of the colonial period, or its economic inconsistency. In this respect, the Soviet model of forced development, based on centralization, planning and the use of the modern sector (industry) to lead the traditional sector (agriculture) has largely permeated the developmentalist ideology of Third World elites haunted by the idea of accumulation and 'catching-up'. This attractiveness has been felt by regimes with as little enthusiasm for socialism as Kemalist Turkey or Nehru's India. It has doubtless been strengthened by a number of tangible and spectacular achievements by the Soviet Union (the modernization of Central Asia, the despatch of the first Sputnik) and by the concrete support given by the USSR to a number of big projects (the Bhilaï, Helwan and El Hadjar steel mills; the Euphrates and Aswan dams). Economic nationalization, legitimized by the fact that its spread was often at the expense of foreign economic interests, greatly contributed to promoting confusion in many countries between nationalization and socialization, between nationalism and socialism. At this level, the statist model appears as a powerful instrument of social mystification.

And yet, while the single-party model and the priority given to heavy industry illustrate the impact of the Soviet reference in the Third World, they are not enough to analyse the specificity of the socio-economic models of the developing countries. Failure to examine the indigenization of the Soviet reference can lead into the trap of believing that it is all simply mimicry.

Indigenization of the Soviet reference seems first of all politically necessary for all non-communist ruling groups trying to keep communist parties from any participation in the exercise of power. Thus rejection of the 'class struggle' becomes a useful means of disqualifying communist parties in societies where cultural representations disparage its use. In some countries, such elimination is effected with the implicit blessing of the USSR. Moreover, in many cases, the formal appropriation of the Soviet reference has more to do with tactical political considerations than with a concern with ideological consistency. With Nasser the choice in favour of 'scientific socialism' was dictated by the concern to promote the National Action Charter against the 'obscurantism' of the Muslim Brotherhood. This choice proved to be all the more 'worthwhile' because Nasser was able to use it to good effect in his diplomatic and military relations with Moscow. In the same country, the adoption of the Soviet development model for heavy industry reflected much less a doctrinal choice in favour of the Soviet system than an acceptance of the evolutionary theses of development through stages put forward by Walt Rostow. Whence the idea of a 'Stalinist–Rostowian' model, referred to by Michel Chatelus, which 'accounts for the illusions, the ideological confusions, the hopes and the limits that the policies of development socialism contained'.[19]

In this respect, and over and beyond the Egyptian example, it has to be observed that today the 'Soviet model' as the supreme example of autocentred development, has many avatars. The productivist myth which inspired the development of heavy industry greatly contributed to obscuring the effects of technological dependence and growing integration into the international division of labour.[20] This accumulation of productive forces, made possible by growing oil rent, was largely achieved at the expense of agricultural production and employment. This explains the current multiplication in Arab countries of 'rectification campaigns' varying in scope but all directed at lessening the restrictions weighing on the private sector, reducing planning or giving priority to agricultural production. In many cases (Egypt, Iraq) this economic reorientation has gone hand in hand with a more or less apparent loosening of relations with the USSR. The era of 'national recovery' against foreign interests having been completed and that of great state investments over, its diplomatic or economic support become less useful. Max Zins, dealing with India, gives a good account in this book of how the gradual modification of economic restrictions by the ruling class may have a negative effect on the future of Indo-Soviet relations.

It must also be observed that reappropriation of the Soviet reference as an instrument of state-building has not been achieved without paradoxes. In most Third World states in which the Soviet experience has inspired state-building, this has been achieved largely at the expense of building the party. In Boumedienne's

Algeria, the lethargy of the single party had the better of the rather unconvincing attempts to breathe new life into and restructure the FLN. At the crucial moment of the launching of the 'Agrarian Revolution', peasant mobilization was more the work of the *walis* (prefects) than of the party commissars. Whence the relative ease with which the militants of the PAGS (*Parti de l'Avant Garde Socialiste*, Socialist Vanguard Party) made up of members of the former Algerian Communist Party succeeded in occupying the political ground opened up by the student volunteer campaign. In Nasserite Egypt, the party served more to neutralize challenges than to mobilize social forces around a political project. Even in countries such as Syria and Iraq, where the primacy of the party over the state is clearly affirmed, the party structure exists and functions only in relation to the army or paramilitary organizations that are continuously being strengthened. This militarization of the party or its subordination to the army or again its 'duplication' by paramilitary organizations is not limited to Arab regimes. In sub-Saharan Africa, it remains to be seen how far the creation of the EWP (Ethiopian Workers' Party) will alter the hegemony of the military over public affairs.

Soviet reference and national affirmation
The influence of the new Third World states on the international system can be measured from their three central goals: to redefine the terms of their relations with the former tutelary powers following their achievement of independence; to build up a regional space favourable to their 'milieu goals' (Wolfers); and to attenuate, individually or collectively, their subordinate position in the international system. At these three levels of action for which its support might be sought, the USSR plays on its ambivalent position of being outside the international system (for the purposes of denouncing its misdeeds or avoiding its responsibilities) and being inside it (for the purpose, in many situations, of offering a concrete alternative). It thus endeavours to present itself as the midwife in the completion of the independence of the new states, helping them maximize their territorial or regional positions, and being the sympathetic ally of countries subject to an unfair international order.

Outside the military sphere, the USSR's contribution has been most significant when foreign capital was being nationalized and a public industrial sector developed. It must, however, be noted that this contribution has been infinitely more substantial in countries that are closely integrated into the international division of labour and politically not very dependent on it (Iraq, India) than among reliable political allies which are heavily dependent on its political and military support (Angola, South Yemen). This apparent contradiction can be explained by the structural rigidity of a Soviet economy better adapted to the realization of 'big operations' than of smaller projects. It is also linked to the direct economic benefits to be derived from its investments (bauxite, steel, phosphates, oil). Finally, it is justified by the fact that in those countries, economic action is the easiest way for it to make its presence felt. That is why, except for the states that are integrated into the CMEA (Vietnam, Cuba), the USSR is fundamentally perceived in the Third World as a supplementary market useful for diversifying trade and not as an alternative trading partner to the market economies. While its help might be sought in carrying out projects with a long-term return or with which the traditional Western partners have refused to become involved, such assistance is less likely to be required once more profitable opportunities appear on the Western market or needs for industrial goods incorporating advanced technology become apparent. Moreover, even if the balance sheet of Soviet economic assistance is much less negative than it is generally said to be in the West, one cannot fail to notice, following M. Bencheikh, a glaring contradiction between the positions of the USSR 'when it deems that it does not benefit from unequal exchange but takes advantage of market prices fixed in the framework of that exchange and when it declares that it is outside unequal exchange but in fact practises it'.[21]

The USSR has compensated for this structural difficulty in getting itself accepted as the preferred economic partner of developing countries, by a capacity to present itself as a diplomatic partner available to use its political and military resources to promote the stabilization of existing local and regional arrangements.

Among states confronted with centrifugal forces (ethnic, political or religious), the USSR enjoys an obvious credibility which cannot fail to enhance the development of its global strategic power.

It is in Africa, where the territorial arrangements are the most fragile, that this perception is probably the strongest. In the space of 20 years, and with growing success, the USSR has lent military support to Zaire, Nigeria, Sudan and Ethiopia. In certain circumstances it has consented to support autonomist or secessionist movements (Kurdistan, Eritrea), but its aid, which is in fact rather parsimonious, has had more to do with the desire to put pressure on a central government with which it was paradoxically seeking good relations than with a real political guarantee to those movements. Even if the invasion of Afghanistan has probably undermined it, this image of a USSR, managing in the name of realism to sacrifice 'revolutionary movements' or local communist parties on the altar of its state interest, is more powerful in the Third World than that of the USSR as a 'hegemonic power'. The constancy of this behaviour, and hence of this image, has in any event been largely borne out recently in the Middle East where the USSR seems never to have succeeded in balancing its support for Syria and the support it gave to the PLO.

The USSR is perceived as a potential ally in the stabilization of territorial arrangements, and thus finds itself being sought out by actors anxious to preserve or modify certain strongly conflict-laden regional balances. But because it is seen more as an ally whose total support is expected than as a political arbiter, the USSR succeeds better in inserting itself into conflicts where the East–West divide is present (Cuba, Middle East) than in regional areas where the issues at stake are not clearly identifiable at the global level (Cyprus, Iran, Iraq).

In their relations with the USSR, Third World states take into consideration two series of elements that are particularly important: their geopolitical relationship with the USSR and the extent of their diplomatic room for manoeuvre.

Geopolitical relationship with the USSR

In any implicit or explicit analysis of the role of the USSR by Third World states it is impossible to omit an assessment of the real or potential threat that any great power can bring to bear on national independence. In this perspective, it can, without much chance of error, be asserted that whether they are far removed from the USSR, or just next door, structures the perceptions of Cuban, Turkish, Vietnamese or Iranian actors.

As Georges Boudarel stresses in chapter 5, the absence of common borders certainly facilitated Vietnam's alliance with the USSR and increased its room for diplomatic manoeuvre in relation to its ally. The possibility of maximizing their relations with Moscow without running the risk of alienating their sovereignty influenced Indian or Cuban leaders to varying degrees, as is evidenced by the impact that a number of military initiatives taken by the USSR in the Third World have had. In her analysis of Soviet–Iraqi relations, Elizabeth Picard stresses how much Soviet support for Ethiopia and the Soviet invasion of Afghanistan contributed to arousing in Baghdad the fear of a Soviet vice squeezing Iraq. The deterioration of Soviet–Iranian relations has, however, recently led the USSR to step up considerably its support for Baghdad in the interminable Gulf War. More remotely, the invasion of Afghanistan provoked relative disquiet in India. But there is nothing mechanical about this 'geopolitical logic'. The hostility of Khomeini's Iran to the USSR is to be explained more by internal political and ideological considerations than by the fear of a Soviet 'invasion'. And in any case Iran under the Shah, like Turkey, always took good care to maintain good bilateral relations with Moscow. Semih Vaner gives a good demonstration of how successive Turkish governments have been able to find in their relations with the USSR implicit support both for their anti-communism and for the pursuit of certain regional objectives (Cyprus).

In this analysis of the geopolitical relationship with the USSR, particular attention must be paid to Asia, where the perception of the USSR is generally constructed in terms of the active interplay of two major regional actors: China and Vietnam. In this book, Françoise Cayrac-Blanchard shows convincingly how states as unreservedly anti-communist as the members of ASEAN have come to see the reality of the 'Soviet threat' in very different ways. Thailand, for example, because of its proximity to Vietnam has a tendency to see in that country the regional agent of the USSR and to find in China a counterweight to what it feels as a Vietnamese hegemony. Conversely, Indonesia, which has to remember the existence of its Chinese minority, always considers China as the main adversary. As a result it is led, for the same reasons as Malaysia, to consider Vietnam as an autonomous agent and to play down the importance of the 'Soviet threat'; all this without the least doctrinal concession over its staunch anti-communism.

That is why, on a continent where representations of the USSR and the play of alliances appear to be heavily conditioned by the Sino-Soviet conflict, the present timid but detectable signs of a normalization of Sino-Soviet relations are bound to have repercussions on the parameters of the image of the USSR in Vietnam or India or among the league of states in ASEAN.

The room for diplomatic manoeuvre

For most Third World states, their relations with the USSR can be judged by their capacity to use the USSR to serve their own ends, work out a possible alternative alliance, and impose themselves as the USSR's natural partner in a given regional power game.

In fact, just as the existence of a modern political culture is something that puts a brake on the maximal use of the Soviet reference, so the capacity of a state to define and pursue 'milieu or possessional goals' (Wolfers) independently of the USSR will modify the content of any alliance it may make with it. Even for such countries as Vietnam and Cuba that are today integrated into the socialist camp, overall foreign policy remains a key point shaping their relations with Moscow. While their integration into the socialist camp undeniably reduces their diplomatic room for manoeuvre, it enables them, within the general parameters of Soviet policy, to secure a solid political–military guarantee, as well as economic assistance (considerable in the case of Cuba). It also gives them scope for political bargaining which, however, the USSR endeavours to reduce, by, for example, seeking to appropriate for itself the Vietnamese success in Cambodia or the Cuban success in Angola.

This essential question of how far an alliance with the USSR is compatible with the pursuit of their own objectives is also posed recurrently about the regional behaviour of India, Syria or Libya. One of the major rules which the USSR has adopted in the Third World is to encourage the new states in all situations with a potential for weakening Western positions, while limiting its commitment wherever the East–West split is not obvious. That is why, while it contributes heavily to strengthening its allies every time a regional imbalance seems likely to harm its own interests (India, Iraq, Syria, Libya), it is always more reserved with regard to allies pursuing questionable territorial goals (Somalia with Ethiopia, Iraq with Iran, Libya with Chad, Syria with Lebanon). It follows that whenever the alliance with the USSR appears to be hampering the pursuit of its own goals, it will be denounced or put on the back-burner. There are, however, exceptions to this rule, which have to do with the greater or lesser capacity of these states to work out alternative alliances or diversify their sources of support. If Iraq was seeking a hegemonic position in the Persian Gulf following the fall of the Shah, through the partial and temporary loosening of its ties with the USSR, it was because it found in France (arms supplier) and Saudi Arabia (moderate political guarantee in the Gulf and source of funds since 1980) alternative partners likely to support its ambitions. Conversely, the reversal of alliances carried out by Somalia in 1977 proved to be infinitely less successful, in so far as the Soviet Union also had another card to play. It is difficult to see how, in current conditions, countries such as Mozambique or Angola could cut themselves off totally from Soviet support despite its heavy-handed and often constraining character. That is why maximization of the goals of a Third World state can truly be secured only when it is able to impose itself on the USSR as the natural partner for which a substitute is hard to find.

At the present time, the most significant example is perhaps that of Syria, which is managing to tie the USSR to the pursuit of its objectives in Lebanon and against the PLO since it has a possible fall-back solution in Washington, whereas Moscow has no fall-back position in the region. Thus, as it strengthens the Syrian regime, thinking by so doing that it is strengthening its own position in the region, Moscow is in fact helping to maximize Damascus' chances in a possible package deal with Washington.

The internalization of the Soviet reference: hypotheses on political discourse

Now that the concept of instrumentalization, which makes it possible to envisage the Soviet reference as an 'off the peg' adjustable and reversible system of power, has been clarified, we need to go further and ask whether this same reference can be converted into a true *mode of political discourse*, that is, into a normative system fixing symbolic forms of legitimacy and constraining ruling elites.[22]

Relying heavily on the framework for expressing political discourse proposed by J. F. Bayart,[23] we will try here to reply to two essential questions: Under what conditions is the Soviet reference able to make itself into the sole mode of political discourse? And, more precisely, under what conditions does the Soviet reference present itself as a privileged way of approaching social discourse and social reality on the basis of one central antagonism?

These apparently abstract questions have a direct bearing on more empirical issues. Posing the problem of whether the idioms contained in the Soviet reference can be turned into an exclusive mode of political discourse amounts to asking under what conditions the use of the Soviet reference ceases to be instrumental and becomes irreversible. Moreover, looking at the place of the Soviet reference in approaches to social discourse and social reality based on the existence of a principal antagonism, amounts to reflecting on the functional specificity of this reference in situations of extreme polarization (civil war or external threat, for example).

Soviet reference, sole mode of discourse?

It is probably in sub-Saharan Africa and more particularly in countries such as Angola, Mozambique (and, to a lesser extent, the Congo and Ethiopia) that the hypothesis of an internalization of the Soviet reference deserves to be examined, because of the combination of factors that have to do both with the internal political dynamics of these states and the global strategic context of which they are part.

In those states that emerged from wars of national liberation supported by the USSR and in which nation-building is going on under conditions that are more difficult than elsewhere, political independence was immediately accompanied by a reference to Marxism–Leninism and reproduction of the Soviet bureaucratic model. This reference to Marxism–Leninism, linked both to the disrepute of African socialisms and the victory of Vietnam in 1975, the Portuguese revolution and the strengthening of the strategic power of the USSR, constitutes a source of 'vanguardist legitimation' mainly for internal purposes but also for external ones ('most advanced stronghold of socialism' facing South Africa, for example). But, because of the lack of in-depth assimilation of Marxism or the inadequacy of reflection on the historical and social reality of the Soviet system, it takes on the form of an 'apparatus ideology', the use of which is easier to derive from the organization of state power. This pattern is established in such countries as Angola, Ethiopia or Mozambique, but is not, however, to be found in the Congo where, since 1963, the Marxist–Leninist reference has been imposed by the intellectual elite and the Brazzaville proletariat on successive ruling groups.[24]

But in all these states the introduction of the Soviet reference following independence was the key event, since, by occupying virtually the whole of the political arena from the very outset, it can compel the actors in this arena (rulers or ruled) to situate themselves exclusively in relation to it. That is why the hypothesis may be advanced that continued use of the Marxist–Leninist reference will be all the better assured when its introduction as the political idiom of the ruling group coincides with independence.

This hypothesis, provisionally borne out in the Congo, is perhaps being verified in Angola and Mozambique. It will in any event help us to stress that the introduction of the Marxist–Leninist reference probably takes on a more pronounced character in these states than in, for example, Somalia, where the abandonment of the Marxist reference following the break with Moscow resulted from its having been introduced late and for reasons of expediency. In this variegated array of Marxist–Leninist references, particular attention should perhaps be paid to Ethiopia where the revolution was introduced into a political arena structured by the pre-existing imperial order. We would need notably to understand why this revolution, claiming to build its political legitimacy on the ruins of an imperial system, nevertheless draws on that same system for nationalist and centralizing referents.

Independently of the time when it is introduced, the Marxist–Leninist reference will be successfully internalized only if competing ideologies for contemporary state power are discredited. But, apart from Islam, which has little impact in the societies mentioned above, and Western liberal values that are sometimes discredited because of their association with external domination, there is hardly any other ideology to replace Marxism–Leninism. Of course, the 'artistic licence' that often surrounds declared ideological choices in Africa is such as to facilitate an eventual dilution of the Marxist–Leninist reference. But to say that is to ignore the precarious position of these states in the international system and their special relationship with the USSR.

In fact, the willingness of the USSR to project its strategic power to meet the expectations of states seeking political and military support reflects its capacity to impose itself in certain circumstances as the best international guarantor of the sovereignty of African states. But, depending on whether it is working in favour of a newly independent state or a state whose sovereignty is well established, the meaning of this guarantee will vary considerably. As a result the content and implications of Soviet and Cuban assistance to Angola are not strictly comparable to those which marked Soviet aid to Somalia, Egypt or Nigeria.

Furthermore, the specificity of the relations of these states with the USSR was reinforced by an international context of increasing bipolarity. In his analysis of Nasserite Egypt, Anouar Abdel-Malek shows how Nasser saw in non-alignment a means of keeping his distance from the USSR, once he had achieved his 'showdown' with the West. He also stresses how much Tito's influence fuelled Nasser's mistrust of the Soviet Union. Finally, he shows that the Cuban and Vietnamese revolutions had a much greater impact on Egypt than the October revolution.[25] This reasoning, which, as to the last two points, was also that of the Algerian FLN, is worth recording so as to compare it with the distinctly different current international situation. In fact, and to the extent that they have both joined the socialist camp, Cuba and Vietnam can no longer continue to be perceived in the same way by other Third World countries. For such countries as Angola, Mozambique and perhaps Ethiopia, Cuba's new place in the socialist camp illustrates the ability of a country to 'save its revolution', in the face of a hostile external environment and to assert its national position within the socialist system.

Such a perception is bound to impel them to analyse non-alignment in a perspective infinitely closer to that of Havana than that of Belgrade. And this is all the more the case since Yugoslavia is no longer seen today as the purveyor of a true anti-blocs diplomatic project. That is why, while the fluidity of the international system rules out making hasty or definitive judgements, it should not prevent us from underlining the implications of a worsening of international tensions, born of superpower antagonism, for the conditions under which the Soviet reference is used.

Soviet reference and 'discourse of war'

If the Soviet reference appears likely to find in some places in sub-Saharan Africa the conditions for its erection into the sole mode of political discourse, it is partly because the discourse that it proposes as a means to mark out 'the universe of the politically thinkable' (Bourdieu) applies to the historical content of conflict experienced by countries like Angola, Ethiopia or Mozambique. By virtue of its qualities of form and the content of its idioms the 'Soviet discourse' paradoxically offers the most appropriate way of talking about political reality. Because it presents itself explicitly as a closed mode of expression in which the political arena, the roles of the actors and the denouement are laid out in advance, this discourse provides ruling groups with the symbolic sources of their legitimation.

The cardinal principle of the 'Soviet discourse' is to formalize, in Manichaean terms, 'the basic contradiction'. This process is necessary before what Bourdieu calls 'the closure effect' can share the political arena. Thus all social and international reality is reduced to an irreducible conflict between 'the people' and 'imperialism', drawing for references on the Leninist grammar based on the fusion of Marxist and military discourse.

From this initial generic expression, the basic premise is then drawn according to which every enemy of the people is necessarily foreign. 'The contradiction between our people and imperialism could not, therefore, be mediated by an internal political force.'[26] This comes out very clearly from the Mozambican discourse to which we refer here to support what we are saying.

As an expression of symbolic mobilization, the discourse will however succeed in reducing the variety of political options only by 'putting into effect regulations enabling the emitter to control the relationship of that discourse with reality'.[27]

In countries such as Angola and Mozambique, this regulation was established and then amplified by the link between the adversaries of the central government (UNITA, MNR) and South Africa. The whole political discourse of these regimes consists in relating all the internal contradictions to this reality by using the inexhaustible resources of Stalinist discourse on 'class infiltration by foreign agents'. Thus, the existence of a social stratum composed of 'aspirants to the bourgeoisie' is explained not by the existence of relations of production favourable to its emergence (which would ruin the self-proclamation of socialism), but by its being 'vulnerable to the insidious action of the enemy'. The latter will be necessarily identified as responsible for economic and commercial malfunctioning (reflected by chronic shortages, for example) since it runs counter to the 'effort of the workers to increase production'.

Already a way of discrediting the internal enemy, the expression of the contradiction between the people and imperialism becomes an instrument to justify external alliances. Thus, not only is there a tendency to justify links with the socialist camp of which the countries feel themselves fully-fledged members, but also to perceive all international reality in terms identical to those used by the USSR. Imperialism, accused of fomenting instability in Southern Africa, will be suspected of seeking to take advantage of Poland's internal problems 'to launch a campaign of subversion and defamation against the socialist community' and of endeavouring 'to overthrow the legitimate revolutionary governments of Afghanistan and Kampuchea'.

Because the absolute 'closure effect' that it seeks remains dependent on the necessary and complete consistency of the internal and external levels, the 'Soviet discourse' systematically excludes the formulation of any 'nuance'. To admit that the reality of the world is not reducible to the antagonism between socialism and capitalism would amount implicitly to admitting that the domestic enemy is not always and everywhere an 'infiltrated agent'.

This discourse, some of whose forms we have outlined here, thus fulfils the essential functions: it mystifies the social and diplomatic arena, provides for political control and helps set up a structure of managerial authority.

Basing the perception of social reality on the confrontation between the people and imperialism makes it possible, through identifying the class enemy with the external enemy, to get around the basic contradiction between the proclamation of socialism, which marks the end of the class struggle, and the survival of this same class enemy. But at the historical stage which these states have reached, the simultaneous expression of the victory of socialism and the persistence of the class struggle is particularly useful. It makes it possible both to block and discredit any questioning of the power of the rulers (since the rulers are socialist, their enemies can only be the enemies of socialism) while using the ideology of class struggle to intensify the regimentation of the ruled. Diplomatically, the verbal denunciation of the antagonism with imperialism makes it possible to mystify both the organic relationship between Marxist–Leninist African countries and the capitalist system of domination, and the quest for a tactical *modus vivendi* with South Africa for example. It may also in some cases partake of the granting of formal commitments to the USSR in order the better to pursue in reality a more independent policy.

The second function of this discourse is to use the symbolic resources of political and military mobilization in order to hasten the regimentation of the population and eliminate 'recalcitrants'. Thus there will be an apologia for repression by transposing into the present the mystique of unity inherited from the war of liberation: 'The weapons with which we fought Portuguese colonialism must be used again to fight the tribalists, the regionalists and the racists . . . Strengthening the revolution in Mozambique will only be achieved with the blood of reactionaries, the blood of each counter-revolutionary will strengthen the revolution'.[28]

Yet, if we accept that it is now essential to take political culture into account as a determinant factor in the international system, its influence remains uncertain. By signing one after the other a non-aggression pact with South Africa and a ceasefire agreement with the MNR, the Mozambican regime is, by its diplomatic behaviour, destroying the whole foundation of its mode of expression based on the reduction of domestic contradictions to the existence of an external threat. It remains then to be seen whether in this case the inevitable reordering of the mode of expression will still be effected through the intermediary of the 'Soviet reference' and whether this will survive a cooling in political relations with the USSR. Beyond the Mozambican example, the response to this question will, perhaps, have a not insignificant influence on the USSR–Third World problematic.

This collective reflection, on which this introductory chapter opens, centred largely on the concept of the instrumentalization of the Soviet reference and its eventual conversion into a mode of political expression cannot exhaust such a complex subject. It simply proposes to bring out, using particular cases, a few research hypotheses which it is to be hoped will stimulate further reflection on this new dimension of international relations.

Notes

1. See P. Wiles, *A New Communist Third World*, London, Croom Helm, 1981.
2. See E. Todd, *La chute finale*, Paris, Laffont, 1976.
3. M. Rodinson, *Marxisme et monde musulman*, Paris, Le Seuil, 1972, p. 314. (Eng. tr. M. Pallis, *Marxism and the Muslim World*, London, Zed Press, 1980).
4. A. Laroui, *L'idéologie arabe contemporaine. Essai critique*, Paris, Maspero, 1967, p. 154.
5. See A. Laroui, *La crise des intellectuels arabes: traditionalisme ou historicisme?*, Paris, Maspero, 1974 (Eng. tr. D. Cammell, *The Crisis of the Arab Intellectual, Traditionalism or Historicism*, Berkeley, University of California Press, 1976).
6. A. Corten, 'Substrats', unpublished article, p. 19, forthcoming in A. Corten et al., *Les autres marxismes réels*. Paris, Bourgois, 1985.
7. See H. Al-Shawi, 'Le contenu de la contestation communiste en Irak et en Syrie', *Maghreb–Machrek*, 63, May–June 1974, pp. 63–75.
8. A. Abdel-Malek, 'Marxisme et libération nationale', in *Centenaire du 'Capital'*, Paris, Mouton, 1969, p. 264.
9. Quoted in A. Abdel-Malek, *La pensée politique arabe contemporaine*, Paris, Le Seuil, 1970 (Eng. tr. M. Pallis, *Contemporary Arab Political Thought*, London, Zed Books, 1983).

10. M. Lowy, *Le marxisme en Amérique Latine*, Paris, Maspero, 1980.

11. G. S. Harris, *The Origins of Communism in Turkey*, Stanford, Hoover Institution Publications, 1967, p. 10.

12. The Maoist reference is often accompanied by an idealization of the Soviet model in its most Stalinist version. See, for Africa, O. Afana, *L'économie de l'Ouest africain. Perspectives de développement*, Paris, Maspero, 1977 (new ed.).

13. On the differences in diplomatic behaviour among African states at the UN on the Afghan question, see Z. Laïdi, 'L'URSS et l'Afrique: vers une extension du système socialiste mondial?', *Politique Etrangère*, 3, 1983, pp. 679–99.

14. See C. Bettelheim and B. Chavance, 'Le stalinisme en tant qu'idéologie du capitalisme d'État', *Temps Modernes*, 393, April 1979, pp. 1757–60.

15. B. Badie, *Culture et Politique*, Paris, Economica, 1983, p. 17.

16. O. Carré and G. Michaud, *Les Frères musulmans d'Égypte et de Syrie*, Paris, Julliard-Gallimard, 1983, p. 21 (Archives).

17. See O. Michaud, 'L'État de Barbarie 1979–1982', *Esprit*, November 1983, pp. 16–35.

18. See R. Lefort *L'Éthiopie: La révolution hérétique*, Paris, Maspero, 1981. (Eng. tr. A. M. Berrett, *Ethiopia, The Heretical Revolution?*, London, Zed Books, 1984.)

19. M. Chatelus, 'Le monde arabe vingt ans après. De l'avant-pétrole à l'après-pétrole. Les économies des pays arabes', *Maghreb-Machrek*, 101, 1983, p. 9.

20. See S. Amin, *Irak et Syrie 1960–1980*, Paris, Minuit, 1982.

21. M. Bencheikh, *Droit international du sous-développement*, Paris, Berger–Levrault, 1983, p. 40.

22. C. Roig, *La grammaire politique de Lénine*, Lausanne, L'Age d'Homme, 1980, p. 181.

23. J. F. Bayart, 'La revanche des sociétés africaines', *Politique Africaine*, 11, September 1983, pp. 123–24.

24. P.-P. Rey, 'Le marxisme en République Populaire du Congo, la société et l'État', unpublished article, p. 3., forthcoming in A. Corten et al., *Les autres marxismes réels*. Paris, Bourgois, 1985.

25. A. Abdel-Malek, *L'Égypte, société militaire*, Paris, Le Seuil, 1962, pp. 229–30.

26. Report of the Central Committee to the IVth Congress of Frelimo, Fr. version in *Mozambique du sous-développement au socialisme*, Paris L'Harmattan, 1983, p. 77. Except where stated, all the citations that follow are drawn from this report. (Eng version: *Out of Underdevelopment to Socialism, Report of the Central Committee*, Maputo, Frelimo Party, 1983, p. 64.)

27. C. Roig, *La grammaire politique de Lénine*, op. cit., p. 135.

28. 'President Machel addresses Quelimane Rally', quoted in *Daily Report, Middle East and Africa*, FBIS, 11 August 1983 (Annexe 027), pp. 45–6.

1 The USSR, Alibi or Instrument for Black African States?

Jean Copans

> *Russia is a great example*
> *for the peoples of the East in revolt.*
> **Radek** (1920)[1]
> *Africans must use Marxism, but*
> *Marxism must not be allowed to use Africans.*
> **Samora Machel**[2]

We have deliberately limited our topic of reflection to a study of the meaning and the practical and ideological role of the USSR in those states claiming to be engaged in social and national liberation. The socialist and Marxist, even Marxist–Leninist, reference of parties, states and leaders will serve as an initial criterion. But while dealing with a matter of current concern, our contribution also seeks to be an urgent appeal for a historical, sociological and political analysis of this vast problem which still remains imprisoned in a rather crude ideological and political straitjacket.

It is not a matter of transforming a pervasive anti-Sovietism into a theoretical tool. It is a matter of going beyond the salutary critique of certain illusions which we shared, and producing the analytical tools for a Marxist analysis of governments claiming to be Marxist without, however, underestimating their specificity. We accept the approach adopted by Daniel Hémery dealing with Vietnam:

> Doubtless when dealing with the Marxisms of the so-called Third World, we need not only to describe their various features and their specificities, but, equally, to ask why they exist, and, as a corollary, why they do not exist . . . , [we need to ask] about the historical conditions and particularities of their emergence, or of their sporadic existence, about the anthropological terrains where they took root and, a question that is no less vital if it is accepted that there is no movement of ideas that is socially neutral, about the nature of the social groups and interests that have produced these Marxisms. On the basis of what profound historical approach, and for what immediate or long-term ends have these social groups become the purveyors or producers of Marxism? It is perhaps not so much the uses made of *Marxism* in the Third World that raise problems but rather the production of specific *Marxisms* which have functioned as so many responses to the crises of non-Western societies.[3]

Ordinary factual knowledge of the communisms, Marxisms, Marxism-Leninisms of Black Africa is only just beginning. And, on this point, our contribution makes no claim to originality. Moreover, the main thing is to remove the ambiguities and contradictions that bestrew studies in this area by raising a question of methodology and perspective that is at once both scientific and political. In fact, more than any other political example, the USSR lends itself to reinterpretation. The political project (the 'model') and the analytical tool (Marxism) intervene directly in the formation of social struggles and the exercise of power. The particularly rich, because complex, relations between social movement and ideology, between social theory and political praxis, between anti-capitalist model and anti-imperialist struggle make the Soviet reference a very useful instrument for analysing a certain African political imagination.

But we must not fall into the trap of outside influence, of mechanisms of mimicry, and of the dialectic of dependence and anti-imperialism. Nor must we lapse into ideology and believe in the sociological and political virtue of words alone. The experience of the study of the 'African socialisms' which have flourished for a quarter of a century has taught us prudence in dealing with the ideological factor. The uncritical admiration of the 1960s was followed by a form of sociological realism (in which all states were seen as identical). In recent years there seems to have been a return to a deeper analysis of the role and origins of 'revolutionary' ideologies. That is why the proposal to examine the idioms and the modes of political expression seem to me to constitute a necessary stage in the analysis of the 'Marxist' African state. In fact the question posed amounts to producing first of all an analysis of the social relations internal to African formations. The social logic of nationalist movements, of post-colonial 'socialist' states, and of the social groups that produce and consume Marxism and Sovietism explain the multiple meanings of the Soviet reference.

My discipline (anthropology, sociology) and my personal position in the Marxist theoretical and political debate lead me to stress and emphasize this endogenous viewpoint. I shall, therefore, reformulate our shared problematic in the following terms: the USSR as catalyst, stake, pretext, symbol, mask for African social and political struggles. This interpretation in no way denies the international dimension of the relations of force nor the specificity of relations among nation-states. I simply observe that, in the African case, the weakness of revolutionary class struggles in colonial times has produced, perhaps more than anywhere else in the world, governments that claim to be Marxist–Leninist (and sometimes to be based on the Soviet model). This historical contradiction must, of course, be explained by the nature of precolonial, colonial and post-colonial social relations and by the form and nature of the intellectual and organizational diffusion of Marxism within the national liberation movements. But the fit between the Soviet message, from Stalin to Gorbachev, and the needs of the bureaucracies or intellectual *petites bourgeoisies* of Black Africa is not the least of paradoxes. Unless one is to think that in return the African use of Marxism–Leninism and the Soviet (or Chinese) model says a great deal about the social constitution of power in the so-called socialist states! It is because the USSR as a *state building socialism in one country* establishes national strategies for political consolidation that its message has so much success with the independent African states. The attractiveness of the model has nothing to do with any aesthetic of politics but everything to do with the social logic of the bureaucratic preservation of clearly defined class interests. To paraphrase Claude Lévi-Strauss: 'The universe of bureaucracies is closed because they talk only to each other.'

Yet the origins of the African image of the international communist movement need to be looked at more closely. This image was to serve as a link between the national interests of the USSR and those of African revolutionary governments. In fact, the earliest Marxist and communist analysis of Africa that we have is of South African . . . and Soviet origin.

The work by A. T. N'Zula, I. I. Potekhin and A. Z. Zusmanovitch[4] marks the beginning of theoretical interest in Black Africa in the circles of the Internationale and its affiliated organizations, as well as in Soviet research. Robin Cohen's excellent introduction to the new edition retraces this whole story. Between 1928 and 1935, it was thus essentially South Africa that represented Black Africa. The existence of a large white working class, the widespread proletarianization of the African population and a duly constituted Communist Party no doubt go a long way to explain this choice. The empirical information is often first hand, but West or Central Africa are not forgotten. Nevertheless, the authors naturally tend to project the image of the black proletariat and the landless peasantry of South Africa on to the rest of Africa (especially as one of the objects of the work is to analyse the effects of the depression). Thus, a first attempt provoked by the most visibly capitalist situation in Black Africa confirms, without problem, but also without too many errors, the orthodox Marxist and communist vision. There is no doubt that this model re-exported elsewhere in Africa was to have disastrous effects.

Once this connection has been established we can develop our study on two distinct levels. We shall first try and analyse the content of the Soviet reference in the national liberation movement, whether struggling or in power; and then examine — unfortunately too superficially — a few detailed cases buttressing our hypothesis.

The Soviet reference in the national liberation movement

The 'political' Africanist literature is very instructive to the extent that goodwill usually replaces Marxist theory. There seem to be two currents, similar in their judgement: that of the fellow-traveller and that of the Third-Worldist activist.

The most important work on the first generation of 'African independence' is that by Yves Bénot.[5] From personal experience, political prudence and the very level of analysis – only ideological discourse – this author's approach passes over the *social reasons* for the use of the Soviet model and praxis. However, Bénot does dare to raise an important problem: that of the impact of Stalinism. He observes:

> Herein lies a first peculiarity, in that while there *are* African Marxists, usually intellectuals, more rarely trade unionists, one would seek in vain for communist *parties* . . . On the whole African continent, there are at most four communist parties, all illegal: one in Morocco . . . , one in Tunisia . . . , a third in Sudan . . . a fourth in South Africa; plus one party that claims to be Marxist–Leninist in Senegal: the African Independence Party. And that is all.[6]

But it is above all his remarks on the 'impact of Stalinism' that deserve to be recalled. Those who were the theoreticians and leaders of the period of the anti-colonial struggle grew up in the time of Stalin. The ability to be dogmatic is perhaps conducive to action but not to the analysis of African realities. But above all the socialist model of development was reduced to the USSR and its 'successes':

> It should be added that Stalinist praxis itself, the methods of managing the single party, controlling information, keeping statistics secret (to mention only three features that we find in independent Africa too) did not fail to impress and seduce African politicians; for those among them who held power, it is easy to understand that such methods appeared very convenient . . .[7]

Basil Davidson, although he has been intimately involved in supporting these movements, *never* mentions these problems in his study of 'the awakening and struggles of African nationalism'![8] This attitude on the part of the fellow-traveller who takes good care not to mention reservations or criticisms, or to produce analyses that might 'play into the enemy's hands' or undermine enthusiastic and wholehearted support, seeks to emphasize the well-foundedness not only of the anti-imperialist strategies but also of the 'national democratic' state constructions.

The position of the Third Worldist activist is often one of simple anti-Stalinism. His radical humanism may lead him to denounce worldwide manipulations and social and political inequalities. Unfortunately, rigour is not his strong suit. Gérard Chaliand once quite rightly denounced the 'revolutionary myths of the Third World'.[9] In his survey of anti-imperialist national revolutions, he put forward a number of sociological analyses of ideological illusionism, the real social nature of ruling classes, and the function of the leader. He noted that the international communist movement's support for the national democratic state[10] leads *de facto* to playing into the hands of the privileged strata: the *petite bourgeoisie* once in power becomes an administrative bureaucracy.

But how to make the link between the Third Worldist or African interests of the Soviet bureaucracy and these regimes with their particular nature? The economist Samir Amin, as always, examines the phenomena globally. To characterize the nature of peripheral capitalism, he has to deal with the national liberation movement. In *Class and Nation*,[11] he declares that 'The fundamental question of our time, to which all other major and minor questions are related, is whether the bourgeoisie is still a rising class.'[12] The predominance of the national liberation movement, which became clear after 1945, enabled the USSR to accede to the rank of world power. Dependent development cannot lead to full capitalism: the internal class struggle is on the agenda. But if Samir Amin condemns the USSR's support for 'national' bourgeoisies, he does so only to take refuge in a Maoist position which he sees as the only truly revolutionary one. We shall leave this new debate aside and simply say that, seen from Black Africa, the replacement of the USSR by China changes nothing in the social logic of class rule and the function of a foreign 'revolutionary' model.

The most recent evocation of a Third Worldist viewpoint is that by Jean Ziegler in *Les Rebelles*.[13] The author touches explicitly on the question of the USSR's relations with the national liberation movement. While there is nothing original about some of his analyses, some interesting suggestions emerge from his unrepentant lyricism. First of all he explains that the USSR has become a superpower defending its own interests in the Third World. But he adds that the new generation of revolutionaries is not fooled by this reality,[14] even though he admits at the same time that no national liberation movement could have been successful without the material and diplomatic aid of the USSR.[15] Later on, Jean Ziegler analyses what he calls 'the mutilation of the national liberation movement: its transformation into a Soviet-type Marxist–Leninist party'.[16] For him, the USSR reproduces the inequality of the capitalist world market. Its political and material support thus involves the local reproduction of the Soviet political machinery (pseudo-democratic centralization, secret police, weight of the military technocracy), even if this dimension cannot hide the social nature of the national liberation movement, both in its practice of struggle and in the social make-up of its leadership.

From there it would perhaps be possible to go on to reflect on the organizational and militant weakness of the autochthonous communist reference, the dual dependence on the Soviet Union and the colonial metropolitan communists,[17] with a dogmatic Marxist theory imposing a double model of analysis of colonial reality and mobilization for 'the construction of socialism'. But these political characteristics only assume their full meaning if they are confronted with the historical conditions of the struggle for national liberation and independence. These generally involve the existence of a privileged leading core made up of officials and intellectuals, the development of a unanimist anti-imperialist ideology opposed to the elucidation of the class nature of the 'national movement', and the presence of an independent state copied directly from the colonial apparatus whose motor remains bureaucratic domination and economic exploitation.

It is thus possible to understand the total absence of reference in practice to Marxist–Leninist ideology which can be summarized in the following dogmatic formula: absence of any materialist and historical analysis of local class relationships (when it is not a pre-capitalist illusionism), plus an ideological (and not sociological) model of the anti-imperialist struggle, plus a Stalinist model of power and mobilization, both party and state.

This situation seems altogether specific. Looking very rapidly at analyses relating to Asia or Latin America one is struck by two phenomena: the existence of mass revolutionary practices in colonial times; and the existence of critical revolutionary practices in the theory of the Stalinist model of bourgeois national liberation.[18] As for the construction of the socialist model, it is true that things are more complex since today models exist in profusion – and confusion. Some even go so far as to say that hardly any models exist any more.

Before concluding this first series of reflections, we should touch on both the colonial and the post-colonial periods since political independence introduced only a difference of degree and not one of nature in the function of the Soviet role.

In fact, the relationship between political space, class struggles and the space of the world capitalist economy always rests on a dual system of determination. The anti-imperialist struggles of yesterday or today remain national political struggles for state power. The relationship between the class position of political leaders and the absence of political democracy rests on social domination and ideological obfuscation. The Soviet model and in some cases the Soviet presence then serve as instruments for consolidating the power of those who *in reality make their national interests prevail*.

The experience of the second generation of socialisms (Ethiopia, Benin, ex-Portuguese colonies, Zimbabwe) confirms this assessment. It even worsens it in some ways to the extent that the achievements of the armed social or national liberation struggle (compared to the compromise independences of the 1960s) do not result in a different practice – a peaceful one – of the political struggle. The resurgence of anti-imperialism as the dominant ideological form is there, too, an original form of obfuscation of internal social contradictions.

Classes and state power

We have already set out elsewhere the voluntary nature of the political silence about social classes and the class struggles around the taking and keeping of power.[19]

Being unable to produce here a theory of the socialist or revolutionary national democratic state, we propose with the help of an analysis of a few examples from the available literature to show the recurrence of the (ruling) class social logic in the Marxist and then Soviet assertion of the discourses and acts of state power.

The primary illusion is that of the neutrality of the state apparatus. The ideological and political cause is held to define the class nature of this state. That this new state is the extension of the colonial apparatus appears to concern our revolutionary theoreticians hardly at all. The argument of the Nigerian activist S. G. Ikoku, a supporter of Kwame Nkrumah's regime, is disturbing in its simplicity:

> It is only through analysis of political power that it is possible to establish the nature of a state-led economy: from the outside, state capitalism and socialism are strangely similar. In both cases we have state enterprises, the crushing of private entrepreneurs and the decisive importance of experts. But there is a basic difference. In the case of socialism, the experts and administrators owe their dominant position to the free choice of the people, a free choice that is periodically reaffirmed . . . And the core of experts works in the framework of the directives and line laid down and controlled by the freely elected representatives of the people.[20]

It would then be enough to claim very loudly a mandate from the people and the revolution in order to defend it . . . And what better sign of the 'class' nature of this state than the verbal if not practical (administrative) invocation of the Soviet model!

The socialist policy of bureaucracies serves to channel some of their interests, and to camouflage those that cannot be admitted. Jean-Loup Amselle, in comments on socialist Mali (1960–68) gives a good account of the 'bourgeois' effects of the 'Leninist' policy in favour of a modern 'collective' agriculture: the state bourgeoisie was to constitute itself into a ruling class on the backs of the peasantry.[21]

I. Bagayogo, who studies this phenomenon more closely, several times mentions the real causes of the socialist orientation: the national interests of the colonial bureaucracy transforming itself into a state bourgeoisie.[22] His description of the experts and militants defending their power by means of state power is unambiguous: 'It is in this perspective that the socialism of the US–RDA must be analysed.'[23]

Thus, the public sector fulfils an economic function and also an ideological function which makes it possible to condemn capitalism and justify the role of national leaders.[24] The existence of a model (the Soviet one) that legitimizes both internally and externally the power of those who occupy state power is an asset that is still brought to bear in Mali today, notably at the level of the organs of repression. It would, of course, be necessary to specify when and how the Soviet example intervenes in this practice, to what extent the reference is spontaneous or suggested (by the USSR itself!). But there is no doubt that the USSR gives credence to a verbal, administrative and repressive practice of building socialism and that this ready-made system is attractive to social categories whose mass bases no longer have the dynamism of national unity.

Several analysts have taken up the expression 'off the peg' model. It may seem somewhat inappropriate to the extent that precisely what is most important to us is the alterations made to the model. Since the advantage of the 'off the peg' is to render these alterations unnecessary, it would be better to grasp the personality of the tailor and his working instruments (measure, scissors, needles, etc.). Immanuel Wallerstein confirms how important the factors of adaptation to the model are when he deems that the Democratic Party of the Ivory Coast (PDCI) functions (supreme paradox!) like a Marxist–Leninist party. In other words, the indigenization of Marxism or the soviet may assume the most unexpected forms.

In his analysis of the contemporary Congo, H. Ossebi confirms this view of the state: 'Public over-administration encloses the "public" labour market in the clientelist sphere of the state apparatus.'[25] Further on he explains the practical content of the chosen ideology:

> By creating the PCT (Congolese Labour Party) the military regime realized a highly significant political operation which enabled it to enclose all ideological stances in a totalizing frame of reference: that of Marxism–Leninism . . . The 'opponents' of this new ideology found themselves as a result placed before the following alternative: either to conform and obey the 'party'; or refuse to do so and be considered as 'reactionary', 'anti-communist', etc.[26]

And the author adds:

> Scientific socialism, national liberation, etc., thus appear here as mythical images offered to the collectivity by a ruling class that takes good care to obfuscate its place and role in the perpetuation of the established order.[27]

This role as a court of appeal, and the legitimizing function played by a foreign state which is both a diplomatic support and a model, becomes even more visible in periods of crisis or conflict. It makes it possible at such times to denounce external enemies more explicitly and to identify internal enemies. These enemies may even be found in the state or party apparatus. There, too, the Soviet model is of great use in the theorizing about internal ideological enemies. Is it not possible to see echoes of the trials of the 'Hitlerite–Trotskyists' in the 1930s in the condemnations of political opponents in Angola or Mozambique? The Ethiopian experience, too, has largely preferred physical elimination to political dialogue.

The cases of Angola and Ethiopia are certainly the most relevant for our project, to the extent that the Soviet and Cuban interventions confirmed the seriousness of the political choices. In addition, the debates concerning the experience of these countries are old and many-faceted.[28]

For Angola, we take on board most of the position taken by Claude Gabriel. His methodological position consists in asking about the social nature of the regime and the policy pursued, going behind official ideological proclamations: indeed without such an effort, it would be impossible to understand why Somalia moved from state capitalism to socialism and then back to state capitalism purely on the strength of its diplomatic and ideological references:[29]

> When it is used in this way Marxism–Leninism becomes nothing more than a propagandist and demagogic schema by the leadership in power to call for discipline and production. Marxism is emptied of all its dialectical substance to justify the present state of political power and to exorcize reality, the reality of a *petit bourgeois* nationalist leadership manipulating the mass movement for the legitimacy of its state power.[30]

In this schema, the USSR's support has obvious implications domestically: 'The political credit and the political and military aid that Moscow dispenses to these neocolonial regimes favour the falsely Bonapartist "above it all" function of governments and facilitates their repression of the vanguard.'[31]

Nito Alves, whose pro-Sovietism seems to have been one of the identifying factors in an internal power struggle, explained in April 1976:

> This whole productive machine, this whole state apparatus, the whole cultural movement can only be conceived in the conditions of functioning of a party like the CPSU . . . That is: the very responsibility of the Party as the leading force necessarily implies the permanent functioning of the central committee.[32]

The Stalinist model thus responds to the ideological needs of the MPLA but it is obvious that the comparison between Angola and the people's democracies[33] cannot be pushed too far.

The debate engaged around these issues in the *Review of African Political Economy* is most enlightening. Paul Fauvet and Basil Davidson defend the Luanda regime by stressing its domestic and external difficulties, and the necessarily *petit bourgeois* nature of its revolutionary leadership (Fauvet gives free rein to his naïveté when he asks 'So what's wrong with Angola that isn't wrong with, say, Vietnam or Cuba?').[34] Tony Southall and W. G. Clarence-Smith[35] put more stress on the reality of class conflicts and the refusal of the MPLA to de-bureacratize the leadership of the mass movement.

Curiously, Jean Ziegler shares this attempt to make a sociological analysis of the MPLA. He observes that unlike the PAIGC or FRELIMO, the MPLA never built a state. It inherited the one abandoned by the Portuguese and was not based on any liberated zone: 'At the moment of the proclamation of independence, no revolutionary counter-society – the embryo of a new society to be born – existed on any part of the territory.'[36] The *petite bourgeoisie* of mestico officials transformed the liberation movement into a Soviet-type one-party state. The absence of mass political practice thus led to the inevitable reproduction of the state logic.

Jean Ziegler, who saw Nito Alves as a leader who was more sensitive to the needs of the masses, does not however explain why his strategy took on a 'pro-Soviet' and 'putschist' content. Although very critical of this latter, Paul Fauvet's very detailed article shows in what way pro-Sovietism was the result of an intra-bureaucratic conflict and hence an issue in the power struggle.[37]   The same leitmotiv runs through Claude Gabriel's description in 1978, Ronaldo Munck's in 1980[38] or Jean Ziegler's in 1983: political problems cannot be settled by administrative measures. The intervention of the masses must be democratically encouraged and organized. Words are no substitute for practice.

The 'revolutionary' practice of Ethiopia is almost of another nature and perhaps unintentionally links up with certain very Stalinist features: the physical liquidation of vanguards and the armed repression of regional autonomy. The pre-eminence of the military marks de facto continuity with the previous regime. For C. Braeckman, this is an imperial socialism,[39] for John Markakis we are witnessing the appearance of a garrison socialism of which Ethiopia is the best example.[40] The violence of revolutionary discourse cannot remake history just as it wants.

'The new masters of Ethiopia have retained the taste for secrecy, centralism and bureaucracy which typified the feudal regime and sits very well with the practices of a socialism imported from East Berlin or Moscow.'[41] The state has not changed, indeed quite the contrary – the militarization of socialism becomes a practice that is not restricted to the political victory of the military. This militarization is the best guarantee of survival both for the Ethiopian leaders and for their Soviet and socialist supporters. The consolidation of (imperial) power goes by way of the affirmation of so-called national unity: in this case, the military solution becomes self-evident, and acquires a *raison d'être*. At the same time, the military technocracy trained in the USSR is much more reliable than the militant turned administrator, technician or intellectual.[42] That is why armed and police repression works better in Ethiopian socialism. Here the USSR is at once a statist, a political, an ideological and a national model. The choice of socialist ideology, and then more precisely of the Soviet variety, has to do with the nature of class conflicts and the social function of the army. There seems to be universal agreement on this point among observers of the Ethiopian revolution.[43]

We have to turn to René Lefort's informed first-class analysis in order to show the play of the mechanisms that leads Marxism and its Soviet usage to be an instrument of social power of a very precise category of soldiers. The agrarian reform, the alliance between the Marxists and the army, the (sought out) support of déclassé urban social categories, the return of senior officers, the *de facto* identification of the party with the army, are all so many episodes that confirm the pragmatic use made of the Soviet reference or Soviet aid.[44] René Lefort considers these soldiers as more nationalist than the previous regime and Soviet aid enables them to save face given that Western aid continues to be much larger.

Quite clearly, the most tragic lesson of the Ethiopian case lies in the area of political democracy: the physical elimination of opponents, the determination to put down the Eritrean problem by military victory amply justify the slowness (the *de facto* refusal) to build a revolutionary party other than by administrative measures. As René Lefort explains:

> The issue was whether the party would be exclusively made up of the military or whether it would include civilians, not as representatives of any mass political organization but purely as individuals. And this decision was mainly debated in terms of the attitude of the Eastern countries which linked the scale of their support to respect for the most elementary forms of socialist regimes. The composition of the party was no longer even a problem of domestic policy; it did not depend on the relations of force between civilians and soldiers within Ethiopian society. *It was wholly linked to the balance of tendencies within the Derg and in the army in general, and to the state of Ethiopia's relations with its socialist allies.*

And the author adds: 'Disguised for purely ideological and diplomatic reasons, the party would be nothing more than an agent of the army.'[45]

C. Braeckman mentions the 1,500 members of the COPWE, whose sociological composition was described by Mengistu in his speech of 3 January 1983: 22% workers, 3.3% peasants and 75% intellectuals, employees, soldiers and other members of society.[46] John Markakis' concept of garrison socialism seems not therefore to be excessive.[47] The Polish experience, making all due allowance, shows that the replacement of the faltering civilian bureaucracy by the army is possible while still continuing to refer to socialism and its Soviet model. The technical, social and ideological advantages of that socialism come to be seen as more important than the democratic image of the revolution. The weight of the military in Soviet society is perhaps not unconnected with these new forms of support.[48]

The social revolution between nationalism and internationalism

In the general conclusion to his book, Zaki Laïdi considers Soviet and American involvement as arbiters of an internal political situation.[49] This arbitration which may contribute to stabilizing internal political arrangements and controlling territorial spaces may be passive or active. In this latter case, it 'is in a position to contribute directly to the structuring of the domestic relations of force'.[50] This hypothesis seems to me to be altogether accurate but I suggested at the beginning of this chapter that it was necessary to go further and examine – as I have tried to do succinctly and at second hand – the social reasons which may lead to the internalization of this arbitrating force. Moreover, in the case of the USSR, this expression is perhaps inadequate: in my opinion it is a matter of class alliances whose diplomatic face is only one of its aspects.

We have suggested taking domestic class relations and the nature of the state as the starting-point for analysis. But, beyond the variety of the cases we have discussed (the Congolese army is not the Ethiopian army), we must get back to the social, ideological and cultural movement known as the national liberation movement. The historical period of these last 40 years is dominated by the taking of national political power in the periphery: 'national' ruling classes, whatever their origins, and whether the causes of their hegemony are conjunctural or structural, have to function in a social space which is not 'natural' to them: ethnic and regionalist clientelism is an expression of these weaknesses and contradictions. There is no national ideology because there is only a nationalist and anti-imperialist history: this process of maturation through opposition to external forces has nothing to do with an internal conceptual and instrumental process of maturation. In short, the ruling class cannot transform the discourse of national liberation into a national ideology. This inability explains the recourse to an ideology with a more social or even socialist content, in cases where 'bourgeois' interests, whether they be indigenous or derive from statist control, are virtually non-existent. Naturally, the nature of the class holding national political power, in this case civilian or military functionaries, needs to be discussed. Is it a *petite bourgeoisie* or a specific bureaucracy?[51]

It remains the case that contemporary African socialist ideology is – by default – the dominant form of national ideology: its abstract institutional and political reference is the only one to short-circuit the interests that are dominant regionally, and put all social categories on the same level. Nationalist ideology is, in its essence – and in its history – bourgeois. The historical genius of the dominant classes in Black Africa is to have understood the impossibility not only of producing but also of using a true nationalist ideology.[52] Finally, the socialist examples, far from being an exception, are seen as expressing the deep meaning of history. The Soviet intervention and the Marxist–Leninist reference correspond more to the new forms of evolution of world capitalism than to an extension – an altogether idealistic and at best verbal extension – of the social revolution, whose foundations, it should be said in passing, have not yet been clearly identified in Black Africa.

Starting from such a perspective, we can talk of 'the trap of socialism in one country'. This national (and nationalist) slogan defined the strategy of building 'socialism' under Stalin: it perfectly fulfilled its function of defending power (those who were in power) and defending frontiers: internal or external regional conflicts are in fact one of the causes of this socialist discourse. Only a national socialist discourse can define an enemy as a class enemy (Somalia or South Africa).

Thus, in order to appreciate the multiplication of socialisms among the front-line states, we need to take into account the national liberation struggle, defence in the face of South African pressure and the alleged effectiveness of a Soviet or socialist model.

Other political questions at once appear as secondary: democracy? the relevance of Marxism–Leninism? the recognition of errors? Of course there is some progress to point to. Thus, there was no ten-year wait to ask how socialism was being built in Zimbabwe.[53] Mozambican self-criticisms give the impression that the criterion of actual practice is seen as more important than the interests of power.[54] But more radical criticisms are rare. African or Africanist intellectuals scarcely dare to stray from well-trodden paths.[55] The debates in the *Review of African Political Economy* often remain tinged with a degree of Euro-centricity.[56]

Yet no subject is taboo any longer. Revolutionary naiveté is no longer fashionable. The pseudo-anti-ethnocentricism of the Stalinists or their successors, as well as that of the Third Worldists, has been defeated: it is no longer possible to say: 'That special socialism is enough for the Blacks: traditional lash, colonial lash, socialist sjambok.' Thank you, we have all given already! The question of the USSR seen by the Third World and particularly by Black Africa cannot be treated independently of the questioning of the Soviet model as *the* model of socialism. Defence of the nation-state against the political democracy of the exploited masses is a social choice and not a political error.

Recourse to the USSR is neither a last resort nor an illusion: it is a powerful instrument of learning about state power for social categories with no experience of the power of the bourgeois nation-state. Ideological coherence, the articulation between control of the masses, the administrative apparatus and police repression have, so it seems, a greater historical efficacy than the bourgeois tradition of the colonial apparatus. That means that there is a class distinction within the various colonial regimes and that the ideological choice is perhaps not so arbitrary as all that. Quite obviously, testing such an hypothesis would require undertaking a true social history of the African national movement: a study of the relations between nationalism (taking power) and internationalism (international class alliances) as a specific form of a social revolution.[57] The strength of nationalism is deliberately to confuse social revolution (change in the dominant social category) and socialist revolution (destruction of the state apparatus by proletarians). We are without doubt in the era of state-building or of the 'over-developed state' in the periphery. But the USSR's policy of 'ideological dumping' exists only because its clients are many. Might a new international division of labour be established: the West getting electrification and the USSR the *soviets*? Yes, but where is the cook in all this?

Notes

1. 'La situation internationale et les tâches des masses ouvrières en Orient', Le premier Congrès des peuples de l'Orient, Baku, 1–8 September 1920, Petrograd, Editions de l'Internationale Communiste, 1921, new facsimile edition, Paris, Maspero, 1971.

2. Quoted by J. S. Saul, 'Mozambique: the new phase', in J. S. Saul, *The State and Revolution in Eastern Africa*, New York, Monthly Review Press, 1979, p. 443.

3. 'Le communisme national au Viêt-nam: l'investissement du marxisme par la pensée nationaliste', in Collectif, *Les aventures du marxisme*, Paris, Syros, 1984, p. 289.

4. *The Working Class Movement and Forced Labour in Negro Africa*, Moscow, Profizdat, 1933. English edition presented by R. Cohen, *Forced Labour in Colonial Africa*, London, Zed Press, 1979.

5. *Idéologies des indépendances africaines*, Paris, Maspero, 1969. In another work, *Indépendances africaines*, Paris, Maspero, 2 vols., 1975, the author repeats, but in a note! (pp. 50–51) the essential part of his argument.

6. Ibid., p. 8.

7. Ibid., pp. 22–23.

8. B. Davidson, *L'Afrique au XXe siècle*, Paris, Jeune Afrique, 1979 (Eng. orig. *Africa in Modern History, The search for a new society*, London, Allen Lane, The Penguin Press, 1978).

9. Paris, Le Seuil, 1976 (Eng tr. *Revolution in the Third World, Myths and Prospects*, Hassocks, Harvester, 1976).

10. Chaliand recalls, p. 187, this marvellous remark by A. Sobolev in the *Nouvelle revue internationale* (February 1965): 'The specific and transitory character of the National Democratic State, is due to the fact that it is not a single-class state, or even a two-class state (workers and peasants); . . . It is a state embodying the interests of the entire patriotic part of the nation which has to repress the overthrown reactionary classes.' Chaliand notes, tongue in cheek, 'that what it was was a republic of boy scouts in which classes would only clash in order to ensure national prosperity better'!

11. *Classe et nation dans l'histoire et la crise contemporaine*, Paris, Minuit, 1979 (Eng. tr. *Class and Nation Historically and in the Present Crisis*, New York, Monthly Review Press, 1979).

12. Ibid., p. 182.

13. *Les rebelles: Contre l'ordre du Monde – Mouvements armés de libération nationale du Tiers monde*, Paris, Le Seuil, 1983. See pp. 295–314.

14. Ibid., p. 54.

15. Ibid., p. 293.

16. Ibid.

17. On this point see C. Liauzu, *Aux origines des Tiers-Mondismes, colonisés et anti-colonialistes en France, 1919–1939*, Paris, L'Harmattan, 1983 and G. Madjarian, *La question coloniale et la politique du PCF 1944–1947*, Paris, Maspero, 1977.

18. See for example, Michael Lowy's introduction to his anthology *Le Marxisme en Amérique Latine*, Paris, Maspero, 1980.

19. J. Copans, *Le concept marxiste de classe: élaborations politiques et théoriques dans le contexte africain et africaniste.* ('The Marxist conception of class: political and theoretical elaboration in the African and Africanist context', *Review of African Political Economy*, 32, April 1985, pp. 25–38.) Colloquium on 'Endogenous groups in world perspective, the imperatives of endogenous development', New Delhi, January 1982.

20. *Le Ghana de N'Krumah*, Paris, Maspero, 1971, p. 53.

21. 'Le Mali socialiste (1960–1968)', *Cahiers d'Etudes Africaines*, 72, XVIII, 4, 1978, pp. 631–34.

22. *Émergence d'une bourgeoisie agraire au Mali: l'exemple des planteurs de la région de Bamako*, 3rd cycle doctoral thesis, Paris, EHESS, 1982.

23. Ibid., p. 111.

24. Ibid., pp. 115–17.

25. *Affirmation ethnique et discours idéologique au Congo. Essai d'interprétation*, 3rd cycle doctoral thesis, Paris, University of Paris V, 1982, p. 75.

26. Ibid., p. 198.

27. Ibid., p. 210.

28. *Angola, Le tournant africain?*, Paris, La Brèche, 1978.

29. See the reply to criticism of his book, 'In defence of the Angolan masses', *Review of African Political Economy*, 19, September–December 1980, pp. 69–74.

30. Ibid., p. 273. C. Gabriel explains very well a few pages earlier (pp. 269–71)

why 'the instrumentalization of Marxism is only the reflection of the historical weaknesses of [these] leaderships'. The shift from 'bourgeois' ideologies to 'socialist' ideologies is to be explained by the maturing of the mass movement, and the structural crisis of the state. The need for new forms of coercion, rationalization and regimentation 'enabled certain African bourgeois regimes to take up for their own account part of the Stalinist ideological system'. John Markakis explains the appearance of a garrison socialism in Ethiopia in this way.

31. Ibid., p. 271.

32. Quoted in C. Gabriel, ibid., p. 333.

33. C. Gabriel, 'In defence of the Angolan masses', op. cit., p. 72.

34. P. Fauvet, 'In defence of the MPLA and the Angola revolution'; B. Davidson, 'Comment on Southall and Gabriel', *Review of African Political Economy*, 15–16, May–December 1979, pp. 148–53.

35. Review of C. Gabriel's book by T. Southall, *Review of African Political Economy*, 14, January–April 1979, pp. 107–10; W. G. Clarence-Smith, 'Further considerations on the MPLA and Angola', *Review of African Political Economy*, 19, September–December 1980, pp. 74–76.

36. *Les rebelles*, op. cit., p. 279. See also pp. 280–84.

37. 'Angola: the rise and fall of Nito Alves', *Review of African Political Economy*, 9, May–August 1978, pp. 88–104.

38. 'Angola – 1980', *Review of African Political Economy*, May–August 1980, pp. 98–102.

39. 'L'Ethiopie ou le socialisme impérial', *Le Monde Diplomatique*, October 1982, pp. 18–21.

40. 'The military state and Ethiopia's path to "Socialism"', *Review of African Political Economy*, 21, May–September 1981, pp. 7–25.

41. C. Braeckman, 'L'Éthiopie ou le socialisme impérial', op. cit., p. 18.

42. J. Markakis, R. Lefort and J. Ziegler strongly stress the role of soldiers trained in the USSR and emphasize their different social origin from that of the officers of the previous regime.

43. See J. Markakis and N. Angelo, *Class and Revolution in Ethiopia*, Nottingham, Spokesman Books, 1978.

44. See in particular the analyses on the following pages: 89–98; 115; 152–53; 167–68; 182; 187; 202; 215–16; 223; 250.

45. Our emphasis, p. 254.

46. See the speech to the second commission for the organization of the COPWE (Commission for the Organization of the Workers' Party) reproduced in English in *Joint Publications Research (Sub-Saharan Africa Report)*, 14 January 1983, pp. 6–28. In September 1984 the COPWE was dissolved and replaced by a new party, the EWP (Ethiopian Workers' Party).

47. This concept is replaced in the practice of socialism 'parachuted' in from on high which is also to be found in Benin, the Congo, Madagascar, Sudan and Somalia. Even though it is a different tradition we must *also* think of the more recent case of Guinea-Bissau for example.

48. See the debate on C. Castoriadis' theses: 'Vers la Stratocratie', *Le Débat*, 12, May 1981, pp. 5–17.

49. *Les contraintes d'une rivalité. Les superpuissants et l'Afrique*, Paris, La Découvère, 1986.

50. Ibid.

51. See the debates on this point in the *Review of African Political Economy* between John Saul, Colin Leys, Judith Marshall and Gavin Williams, etc.

52. If one looks more closely at the dominant ideologies in the 'bourgeois' neocolonial states one is struck by the weight of religious ideologies and specific socio-ideological constructions: the peasant in the Ivory Coast, authenticity in Zaire, etc. Nationalism is not statist democratic liberalism. See the contents of the review *Social Change and Development*, edited by N. Moyo.

53. See *Review of African Political Economy*, 18, May–August 1980, notably the articles by Lionel Cliffe, Joshua Mpofu and Barry Munslow, 'Nationalist politics in Zimbabwe: the 1980 elections and beyond' and P. Yates, 'The prospects for socialist transition in Zimbabwe'. See also B. Munslow, 'Zimbabwe's emerging African bourgeoisie', *Review of African Political Economy*, 19, September–December 1980, pp. 63–69. The announcement of the creation of a Marxist–Leninist party in April 1983 is one of the classical symptoms of the present crisis. The ZANU congress held in August 1984 declared itself in favour of the introduction of a one-party regime.

54. See 'Le rapport au Comité central du FRELIMO présenté par Samora Machel au IV Congrès, le 26 avril 1983', in *Mozambique, Du sous-développement au socialisme*, Paris, L'Harmattan, 1983 (In English as *Out of Underdevelopment to Socialism*, Maputo, Frelimo Party, 1983).

For anyone who wants to judge the 'resurgence' of Stalinist platitudes, this speech is a little goldmine: heavy industry, heroes of labour, failures due to the enemies of socialism, role of the security services are themes which will give a lot of pleasure to connoisseurs.

55. Even the recently founded *Journal of African Marxists* is rather dogmatic. However, a letter from K. Kipenda stands out by the relevance of his comments, August 1982, no. 2, pp. 102–6.

56. See also the Leeds seminar on the 'Transition to socialism in Africa'. Report by R. Meunier in *Politique Africaine*, 9, March 1983, pp. 93–94. See no. 25 of the *Review of African Political Economy*, and B. Munslow, *Africa: Problems of the Transition to Socialism*, London, Zed Books, 1986.

57. I refer to Immanuel Wallerstein's stimulating reflections on the nature and limits of 'anti-systemic movements': social movements and national movements. See for example, *The future of the world economy*, in T. K. Hopkins and I. Wallerstein (eds.), *Processes of the World-System*, P.E.W.S., Annals, no. 3, Beverly Hills, Sage, 1980, pp. 167–80 and 'Nationalism and the world transition to socialism: is there a crisis?', 12 pp. roneo. An extract from this latter will give the tone: 'What I believe is new today is the assertion of the position that the social movements in question had never been social movements at all, but in fact were essentially national movements' (p. 4). (The paper was published in *The Politics of the World-Economy, The States, the Movements and the Civilization. Essays by I. Wallerstein*, Cambridge University Press, 1984; the quotation is on p. 126. Tr.).

2 The USSR as seen by the Ba'thists of Iraq and Syria: Ally or Threat?

Elizabeth Picard

Seen from a Third World country, the image of the USSR varies quite considerably depending on whether one is a rich businessman or a farm labourer, whether one is locked up in one of the regime's prisons or a minister. Even limiting ourselves to the 1970s and only the Iraqi and Syrian cases, the representations of the Soviet Union form a kaleidoscope with countless pieces. The theme we have decided to look at in this chapter concerns only the vision that men in power in these two states reflect and purvey and to which they react. The study is centred on a few dozen leaders of the government, the Ba'th party, the army and the police, and more particularly on a dozen or so individuals, the immediate associates of General Assad, the Syrian head of state since November 1970[1] and those in Baghdad around Saddam Hussein, the strongman of the Iraqi revolution of 1968.[2] In the process of forming the image of the USSR these leaders have to take account not only of the internal situation in their country, but also of regional factors, since the Ba'thist political systems in Iraq and Syria are articulated on the Arab 'national' system. They are thus heirs to a historical and cultural heritage, geo-strategic factors, and ideological influences, whether convergent or antagonistic, which are acting on their environment.

These factors will be presented in the first part; then we shall examine the positive image of the USSR that has gradually taken shape in Iraq and Syria, that of an ally, and in some respects a model, and then look at the limits and negative features of this image.[3]

The features of the picture

For Iraq and Syria, as for the other Arab states in the Middle East, the USSR became politically important only quite recently, after the Second World War. A shield made up of the countries of the 'Northern tier', Turkey and Iran, separates them from it and protects them from a possible threat coming from direct contact with the great power.[4] But the distance between them and Russia/the USSR was more political than geographical since the Ottoman Empire and later the European mandatory powers acted as a screen between the Arab provinces and the rest of the world. Until 1943, it was rather national-socialist Germany that represented for Arab militants both a model and an ally in the struggle against French and British imperialisms.[5]

To this geographical and political distance must be added the hostility between (orthodox) Sunni Islam, the religion of over 45% of the population of Iraq and over 65% of that of Syria, and communism: this is an ideological opposition where each totally excludes the other, but also in the sphere of activism, in particular through the rivalry between the Muslim Brothers and the communists. At first sight, this antagonism had a negative effect on the image of the Soviet Union in these countries, the Soviet Union being the centre of world communism. In fact, this image was to be much more nuanced, in terms of the numerous social and cultural variations within Iraqi and Syrian societies.[6]

Following the victory over nazism, precisely because of the part played by the USSR in that victory, a positive image of the USSR began to take shape in nationalist circles in the Middle East, an image put about particularly by the communists but also by the members of certain ethnic and religious minorities. First, the Orthodox Christians, who represent only 6% of the population of Syria, and less than 1% of that of Iraq,[7] but have played an important role in the Arab nationalist movement.[8] Second, the Armenians, linked by numerous family ties with Soviet Armenia. And above all the Kurds, 7% of the population of Syria, one-third of that of Iraq, who receive, as in Iran, the support of the USSR in their national struggle and on whom the Kurdish regions of Armenia and Georgia act as a focus of attraction, notably because of the place they give to Kurdish national culture.[9] Generally, members of ethnic and religious minorities are attracted to the secular model of the Soviet republics, which rejects any division among citizens of various categories. It must be noted that both the Syrian leaders after 1966 and those of Ba'thist Iraq since 1968 belong to demographically minority communities which have captured political power within the country, precisely in the name of a secular state model: in Damascus the heterodox Shi'ite minority of the Alawites (11% of the population of Syria) and in Baghdad the group of Sunni Arabs (17% of the population of Iraq).

Members of ethnic and religious minorities in each of the two countries played an important role in 1925–35 in the birth of communist parties, closely linked to the USSR in the case of Syria,[10] more independent in the case of Iraq.[11] Of course, it must not be forgotten that the two communist parties were marginal, until the 1950s, nor that the labour movement in the two countries was very weak in terms of both numbers and organization.[12] However, they were both closely allied to the Arab nationalist movement in the struggle for the political independence of the country and the overthrow of the conservative oligarchies linked to the former colonial power, in 1955–58 in the case of Syria, and at the time of the 1958 revolution in Iraq. In order to wage this struggle, they advocated recourse to help from the Soviet Union, as a SLCP (Syrian–Lebanese Communist Party) pamphlet published in 1943 called for:

> Why bother with the country of the Soviets? It is a strange land and remote from us . . . we, on our side, approach this issue as patriots and as Arabs . . . Independence for the peoples and freedom for the nationalities . . . are of the nature of the Soviet state . . . As patriots and as Arabs we must, therefore, adopt an unequivocal attitude towards the Soviet state.[13]

It would be wrong to treat this text as just another stereotyped piece by pro-

Soviet communist party militants. The image of a USSR as the champion of the colonized peoples was shared by the majority of nationalist militants at the time America was taking over in the traditional French and British spheres of influence: Point IV (24 January 1949), Joint Defence Pact (13 October 1951), Baghdad Pact (24 February 1955), Eisenhower doctrine (5 January 1957). The efforts by the United States to bring Syria into a pro-Western alliance were stepped up – Iraq was still a monarchy under British control – alternating with proven attempts to destabilize the government in Damascus, launched from Beirut or Baghdad.[14] But the Western offers, combined with various sorts of pressure, were ill-received both by the liberal bourgeoisie that was governing Syria up to 1963 (except for the Nasserite period of the United Arab Republic, 1958–61), and by the revolutionary leader Kassem in Iraq after July 1958. This was all the more so because the peoples of the Middle East remained deaf to the themes developed during the Cold War, of the communist threat and Soviet expansionism. Quite the contrary, for more than a decade, the Soviet Union represented for the political elites, and for the scientific and cultural elites of the region as well, an unrivalled magnet: it was both an example for the future of the Third World and an understanding about present difficulties in a way the West had never been. In fact, the attractiveness operated even among the popular strata, and the first ambassador from the Soviet Union to Iraq was welcomed in Baghdad in 1958 by an enthusiastic crowd over 100,000 strong.[15] A rapprochement with the USSR was perceived by Arab leaders at that time as the means of escaping an exclusive dependence on the West, particularly in the area of arms supplies: after the contract with Egypt, Moscow signed an arms delivery agreement with Syria in February 1956. On the other hand, the development of non-alignment in the Arab world promoted the dissemination of a positive image of the Soviet Union, as Michel Aflaq, the founder of the Ba'th party, himself explained:

> The policy which weighs heavily on the affairs of the Arabs is the policy of the two Anglo-Saxon states, Britain and the United States. Nothing can equal this policy in impact and force and counter-balance its danger except the policy of a great country which has always been on guard against the designs of British and American imperialism: the Soviet Union. One of the simplest political rules and the first national duty of the governments that are conscious of the interest of their countries, governments which are free to take their stands internationally, is to fight their enemies with the help of the enemies of their enemies, or at least to use them as a threat . . .[16]

The need to turn to the USSR to fight the enemy, or at least to 'use it as a threat' is all the more comprehensible on the part of governments in Damascus and, since 1958, in Baghdad, because their neighbours on all sides, Turkey, Iran, Lebanon, Israel, Jordan and Saudi Arabia were allies of the Western 'camp' which backed them in every little local dispute, be it about trade, borders or whatever. It is to be explained above all by the birth and deepening of the Arab–Israeli conflict after the Second World War, with the creation of the State of Israel after the partition of Palestine in 1947, and the 1948 war. The diplomatic, military and financial support given by Great Britain and France to a state that the Arabs consider an outside excrescence and an aggressor culminated in the tripartite aggression of 1956 against Egypt. Then, after June 1967, the United States took over from the Europeans and granted ever-increasing aid to this Israeli ally whose strategic interests complement their own, and which became the leading military power in the region. During this whole period, the Palestinian question constituted the litmus test by which the Arabs would distinguish their allies from their enemies, by how they stood on the Middle East conflict.

Confronted with what they felt as a concrete threat to the integrity of their countries and the stability of their governments, the Arab leaders, and in particular those of Iraq and Syria, turned to the USSR, with the intention of reversing a balance of power that was unfavourable to them, but also with the aim of finding aid for their projects. The image of the USSR changed in fact from being neutral to being clearly positive during this period. The support it had accorded at its birth to an Israel that it expected to see become a bastion of socialism in a reactionary Middle East remained a subject of reproach from the Arab world whenever the slightest tension arose, but counted for little compared with the need to have the USSR as an ally.

A 'revolutionary and responsible' partner

After 1963 in Damascus and 1968 in Baghdad, the domestic stance of Syria and Iraq, and rising regional tensions, led the two states to draw closer to the Soviet Union. Cooperation with the socialist states developed and by doing so revealed how similar were the analyses of the international and regional situation made by Moscow and the Ba'thist leaderships.

At that time, the Soviet Union gave particularly significant aid in strategic sectors of the economies of Iraq and Syria. First, because the two countries were attempting to make a break with the world capitalist system by embarking on an agrarian reform, nationalizing mining and industry and adopting planning. This 'Arab socialism' whose validity was recognized at the time by Soviet commentators,[17] involved initiating vast infrastructural works which were designed to enable these states to make an economic 'take-off' and escape from dependence. The West had refused financial and technological assistance to these projects which were to form the backbone of the new economy in Syria and Iraq, and the Soviet Union stepped in to give it to them, as it had to Egypt, on favourable terms.

The Euphrates dam, the second largest in the Middle East, was Syria's biggest project of the 1960s and 1970s: a doubling of the irrigated area, making 640,000 new hectares, and production of two billion kWh p.a.[18] West Germany had studied the project, but financing was refused after the Ba'th came to power; the USSR stepped in and signed a technical and financial assistance agreement with the party 'radicals' in April 1966 envisaging a loan of $450 million, one-third of the cost of the works, repayable over 12 years at an annual interest rate of 2.5%. The Tabqa dam was inaugurated in 1973, and, like other major achievements of the Syrian regime – extension of the ports of Latakia and Tartous, development of the rail network – it can be credited to cooperation with the USSR.

For Iraq, it was in the oil sector that Soviet aid was decisive.[19] By agreeing to purchase up to $144 million a year of oil exports (14 August 1970), the USSR gave it the means to stand up to the Iraq Petroleum Company, hitherto the sole concessionaire, and even to nationalize it (1 June 1972). It then agreed to raise its purchases of oil to three million tons a year in the event of a Western boycott and, above all, provided drilling equipment along with loans for the exploitation of the Northern Rumeïla oilfield, and the building of a pipeline linking it to Basra (1970) and a refinery there.

In the years that followed the completion of the Euphrates dam in Syria and the nationalization of the oil industry in Iraq, both countries experienced strong growth. This success, which was also partly due to a favourable international conjuncture – the first oil boom – was credited in both countries to the Ba'thist regimes and their cooperation with the USSR. But the USSR was not appreciated solely for its instrumental role. It was also important in the process of consolidating the Ba'thist governments domestically. The regimes of Syria and Iraq were the result of military coups carried out in a particularly fluid situation, and initially rested on a very narrow support base. The problem of developing their legitimacy and authority was their central concern, particularly faced with a communist party which appeared as a rival to the Ba'th because it addressed basically the same urban educated middle classes. The Soviet guarantee for the Ba'th's socialism thus helped to calm the ideological debate, and quieten the criticism from the domestic left,[20] and, even better, to form Fronts around the ruling Ba'th Party.

On the other hand, the Ba'thist regimes in quest of legitimacy and authority were inspired by the Soviet system of organizing society. The officials of the internal security apparatus in Iraq and Syria were trained by technical assistance personnel from the socialist countries, where they attended courses. The whole of the media was in the hands of a ministry of 'Culture and National Guidance' which made plentiful use of them. While the Ba'th Party was not a 'single' party, it was recognized as the 'leading' one and the only one empowered to recruit in schools, universities and the army. Finally, the number of so-called 'popular' organizations, of youth, women, peasants, etc. linked to the Ba'th Party rose, and the trade unions abandoned their function of making demands and became a transmission belt for the regime. In this sense, one can talk of the influence on the regimes in Iraq and Syria of the 'Soviet model' of rationalization and authoritarian modernization, in which the excessive growth of the state goes hand in hand with a voluntarist official discourse on 'the state representing the masses'.[21]

We have seen that relations between the Soviet Union and the Ba'thist regime in Damascus took a distinctly positive turn with the arrival in power of the 'Marxist' wing of the Ba'th Party in 1966, and the acceleration of socialist measures and nationalization in Syria: economic and trade agreements, arms supplies, etc. The tangible sign of this new warmth was the return to his country of the leader of the CPS (Communist Party of Syria) Khalid Baqdash, who had been living in Prague since 1958, and the entry, also in 1966, of three communist ministers into the government. Would the 'rectification' carried out by General Assad in November 1970, marking a sharp shift to the right, put an end to the good relations between the Ba'th and the Soviet Union? After a period of indecision, the two parties recognized the priority of their alliance over their differences. For Moscow, it was important to preserve a network of cooperation, even a rather loose one, with the progressive regimes in the Middle East; for General Assad, it was important to keep the Communist Party inside the governmental coalition, deprive it of its capacity – however limited – to challenge the government and even to use the communists to widen his own support base. This was the main reason for the creation, in March 1972, of the PNF (Progressive National Front) which the USSR strongly encouraged the CPS to join with three other small socialist parties, despite the fact that the Ba'th gave itself the majority in it (9 seats out of 17) and reserved for itself the sole right to propagandize in the armed forces and among students. The CPS remained too weak numerically and too dependent on the Soviet centre to push the challenge beyond a few criticisms in a press whose circulation remained *de facto* banned.[22] In addition, after 1970, internal divisions between 'pro-Soviets' and 'nationalists' weakened it even more,[23] whereas the Ba'th retained privileged Party to Party relations with the CPSU.

The Soviet support sought by General Assad's regime was thus instrumental throughout the 1970s. At first, it helped him consolidate his regime and secure for himself the support of the socialist and communist forces in the country. Later, this same support enabled him indirectly to neutralize his opponents, and to carry out harsh repression against both the communists and trade union militants in 1979 and 1980.

The need of the Ba'thist leaders in Iraq to retain the support of the Soviet Union during the early years of the regime (1968–75) was even more apparent. The group, to which Hassan el-Bakr and Saddam Hussein belonged, that seized power was a minority in the country, battling with rival factions and above all threatened by the two great sources of challenges, both backed by the USSR: the Kurds and the ICP. As regards the Kurdish rebellion, the Ba'th got the USSR to halt its aid to Barzani, who, after 1970, became a client of the Shah of Iran and the United States. Even better, it received the seal of approval from Moscow for the 'Law on local autonomy' (March 1974) which applied to Kurdistan. As for the Communist Party, whose dynamism and popularity led it to demand a share in power, the Iraqi Ba'th, like the Syrian Ba'th, resorted to the tactic of collaboration by offering it a place in the government and within a National Progressive Front. Long and difficult negotiations resulted in the signing of the National Action Charter (July 1973) to which the Soviet Union gave its approval, apparently indifferent to the restrictions it placed on the militant activities of the ICP in the army, the trade unions and student circles.

Alliance

If the USSR's instrumental aid was essential in implementing development projects and strengthening the legitimacy of the regimes internally, it was indispensable for Syria and Iraq in a bipolar regional and international context. But here it is necessary to put aside the global perspective used in many studies of Soviet policy in the Middle East[24] and adopt the perspective of the Ba'thist regimes.

It has to be recognized that it was not the rivalry between two universally antagonistic ideological, economic and political systems, but rather the immediate threat represented by the possibility of aggression by a militarily superior neighbour that worried the Ba'thist leaders in Damascus and Baghdad. That neighbour was Israel, which was occupying the Syrian province of Kuneitra (the Golan Heights) after 1967, and again advanced in the direction of the Syrian capital during the October war of 1973, while its army was wreaking destruction in Syria costing an amount equivalent to the country's GNP. For Iraq, until the destruction by Israel of the Tammûz nuclear centre in June 1981, the Israeli threat seemed less immediate, although the country stood shoulder to shoulder with the other Arab states. The threat came rather from the rising power of Iran, with its publicly declared ambition of becoming the 'guardian of the security of the Gulf', the annexation in November 1971 of the islands of the Tombs and Abu Musa, and the support it was giving to the Kurds in Iraq.

At first glance, the Ba'thists' calculation was simple: since Israel and Iran were specially close allies of the United States, which was providing them with enormous quantities of weapons, the right course was to turn to the Soviet Union. For diplomatic support, but above all for supplies of weapons and, at a later stage, military assistance in the event of aggression. It seemed quite clear at that time that the USSR, which had signed a Treaty of Alliance with Egypt in 1970 and given it vital help during the war of attrition along the Suez Canal, was ready to commit itself in the region. Saddam Hussein at once saw how useful this could be for his country. General Assad did so for his too, with some reservations.

Following a series of economic, commercial and technical cooperation agreements signed in 1969 and 1970,[25] came a first military agreement between Ba'thist Iraq and the Soviet Union (17 December 1971), which was the prelude to the Treaty of Friendship and Cooperation of 9 April 1972. This was hailed in Baghdad as 'a strategic and ideological alliance between two regimes bound together by a shared revolutionary project, against Zionism and Western imperialism'.[26] Like the treaty with Egypt, it was explicitly defensive[27] and was accompanied by a stepping-up of Soviet military deliveries to Iraq, as well as bilateral consultations: from this time, Saddam Hussein visited Moscow almost every year[28] and welcomed high-ranking Soviet missions in Baghdad, signs of the closeness of relations between the two countries in a period when they were not put to the test.

The alliance between Syria and the Soviet Union developed more slowly during the 1970s, rather unevenly as the need for it became gradually more pressing. After the June 1967 defeat and the loss of the Golan Heights, Syrian–Soviet cooperation took the form of close and frequent consultations, including at the highest level.[29] There were difficult, even stormy, negotiations bearing principally on growing demands by Damascus for sophisticated weaponry to which Moscow only agreed with considerable reservations. A military cooperation agreement was signed on 12 May 1972, and following the October 1973 war, major arms deliveries enabled Syria to rebuild its potential, receive Mig-23s and even reschedule its debt. The following year, deliveries were slowed down because Damascus was pursuing a war of attrition on the Golan Heights which Moscow opposed: they resumed after the signing of the Syrian–Israeli disengagement agreement in Geneva on 31 May 1974. Abundant new deliveries began after the second Egyptian–Israeli agreement of

September 1975, because Syria found itself the sole pivot of 'Steadfastness' towards Israel; a new suspension followed the Syrian–Palestinian clashes in Lebanon between April and September 1976.[30] Between 1978 and 1979, Syrian demands became insistent. Mustapha Tlass, Minister of Defence, and Hikmet Chehabi, Chief of Staff, followed each other to the Soviet capital to ask the Soviet Union to restore the balance of forces facing Israel, now that Egypt had broken with Arab solidarity. Syria paid cash, in hard currencies,[31] for its purchases, and events in Lebanon – Israel's invasion of the south in April 1978, the strengthening of relations between the Phalangists and the Israelis – made it very much afraid that a new war might start. It seems that the Soviet Union then made the provision of new arms supplies to Syria conditional upon reconciliation with Iraq which would put an end to Syrian isolation on the 'eastern front', an isolation which the financial and verbal support of Libya was not enough to break. But the Syrian–Iraqi honeymoon and the proposal for a union of the two Ba'thist states lasted only eight months (November 1978–July 1979), and, in the following summer, Syria suffered serious air reverses from Israeli fighters over Lebanese territory.[32]

Damascus' hesitations about tying itself to the USSR through a treaty similar to that with Egypt and Iraq, its obstinate opposition to Soviet requests for naval facilities in the ports of Tartous and Latakia, were swept aside by the urgency of the situation. On 8 October 1980, General Assad signed a Treaty of Friendship and Cooperation, similar to the Soviet–Iraqi treaty, even though Damascus described it beforehand as 'totally different'[33] from the other USSR and Arab states' treaties. It had the same defensive character (article 6) and was to be the beginning 'of a restoration of the strategic balance in the Middle East'.[34]

At the time, commentators wondered about the significance of the treaty with the Soviet Union, and in particular about the motivations and goals of the Syrian Ba'thists in signing a document when it was known what the Egyptians had done with it and what the Iraqis were thinking about it. Had they paid lip-service to the USSR to ensure their supply of weapons, which continued to lag behind Israel's, or had they obtained a real Soviet commitment alongside them, which would significantly modify the balance of power in the Middle East?

In the period that followed, the ups and downs of Syrian–Soviet cooperation revealed Damascus' dependence on its ally and above all its high expectations of it. The May 1981 'missile crisis'[35] seemed to indicate a change, both qualitative and quantitative, in the USSR's support for Syria. This change was confirmed by the rapid build-up in the number of military advisers: 1,000–1,500 in 1980, 3,000 in 1982 and over 6,000 in 1983. Then, after November 1982, the USSR massively re-equipped the Syrian army, which had suffered very heavy losses in Lebanon during June and July, and more importantly, it set up two SA-5 missile bases under its exclusive control around Damascus.[36] Certain very confident statements by ministers in the Syrian government[37] contributed further to give Syrian–Soviet relations a positive image, positive and satisfactory, that is, for the Ba'thist leaders.

And yet, listing the points of divergence and even disagreement, especially those of a strategic nature, between the USSR and the Ba'thist regimes in Syria and Iraq, it is easy to see that the leaders in Damascus and Baghdad had a more ambivalent and less enthusiastic image of their Soviet ally. This can be observed in both countries, but here we shall look at the Syrian example because it touches on the central problem of the Middle East region: the Arab–Israeli conflict. The Iraqi case will then serve to study the deterioration of relations between the Ba'thists and the Soviets during the decade, in relation to the international context and even more to the domestic evolution of Saddam Hussein's regime.

The image becomes tarnished

After having mentioned the Soviet support for Syria during the crisis of the spring of 1981 and above all the USSR's exceptional commitment to the defence of Syrian territory and even of the Syrian army in Lebanon in 1983, we must attempt to answer the very vexed question of the reasons for the rapid and costly defeat of the Syrian forces in the Beqaa valley and the Lebanese Chouf between 6 and 11 June 1982.[38] What is the Syrian argument? In a diplomatic and veiled manner at the top,[39] simply and indignantly at the popular level, the judgement follows the explanation given in the Western media, according to which the arms supplied by the Soviets to their Arab allies were overcome by Israeli–American technology[40] and/or that the USSR refused to sell its Arab allies the latest equipment. This explanation has its limits. It is notably rejected by the Soviets themselves: they expressed surprise at the immediate withdrawal by Syrian troops in the Lebanese mountains and apparently had their offer of a more direct commitment at the time turned down. Whatever the case, before the General Congress of Trade Unions, on 20 November 1982, Hafez al-Assad, who had returned the evening before from Leonid Brezhnev's funeral, rather blamed the Egyptians, claiming that they had communicated information on Soviet equipment to the Israelis.[41]

However that may be, the accusation remains, and has become louder since 1967: the USSR provides its allies with weapons to fight, to defend themselves sometimes but not to win. It was developed by the extreme left which criticized the USSR for having assisted in the birth of Israel and voted for Security Council resolution 242 in 1967.[42] It was taken up by Islamic opponents who do not forgive Moscow for having allowed several hundred Soviet Jews to emigrate to Israel in the 1960s as part of the programme to reunite families, and systematically stress the Eastern European origin of the leading state figures in Jerusalem. Within the Ba'thist ruling group, these negative images with anti-Semitic overtones were allowed to circulate without displeasure, but the behaviour of the USSR as a 'great power' is the primary object of criticisms.

Because of its obstinate search for a negotiated peace in the Middle East, the USSR is accused of abandoning its revolutionary ideals in order to give priority to defending its own interests, in association with the Geneva disarmament negotiations. Thus, it did not hesitate to distance itself from its local allies, to publish a joint communiqué with the United States (November 1977) and to put forward its own proposals for a settlement (Brezhnev plan of February 1981). But the Syrians are rather hostile to a negotiated settlement as long as there continues to be a strategic imbalance between them and the Israelis.[43] As for the Iraqis, they have only come round to it since 1981, because of their military difficulties with Iran.

On the other hand, in order to advance the solution they advocate, the Soviets are favourable to cooperation among their progressive allies in the Middle East region, which they would like to see adopt a joint strategic line and coordinate their efforts in the Steadfastness Front. Since 1975, the year when the Lebanon conflict got under way, they have been pressing the Palestinians and Syrians to harmonize their positions [44] and openly show their reservations about the hegemonic ambitions of General Assad over Greater Syria (Syria, Jordan, Palestine and Lebanon).[45] These requests are resented by the local actors, and in particular by the governments, as interference and in particular as the mark of the Soviet Union's lack of comprehension of the specific problems of the region.

This disagreement on the solution to the conflicts in the Middle East marks a limit to the consensus between the USSR and its allies. The fact is that the USSR, although accused of pursuing goals of 'destabilization', supports the coexistence of all the states in the region, including Israel, and also the creation of a PLO state in the West Bank, which is not the case with the Syrian Ba'thists in the Corrective Movement who are seeking to redraw the map to their advantage. And it is rather to the United States that Syria seems to be looking for support for its ambitions, recognition of the Lebanese advantages it has seized and a lessening of Israeli pressures from the Golan Heights. There is frequent mention of the convergence of Israeli and Syrian objectives in Lebanon. One of the essential aspects of this convergence lies in the dialogue between Syria and the United States kept up through all the ups and downs,[46] which marks the *de facto* participation of the Ba'thists in negotiations under American auspices. There thus exists a clear difference of degree between the American–Israeli 'strategic consensus', which on the one side is indissoluble, and, until proof of the contrary, open-ended, and on the other, the alliance between the Soviet Union and the Alawite Ba'thist regime in Syria, a contingent, tactical alliance, which it would be hazardous to describe as irreversible.

Questions about the nature of the ties between Syria and the USSR and the validity of the Soviet model of development appeared in 1984 at the heart of the controversy dividing the leaders of the 'Corrective Movement': for some, such as Rif'at al-Assad, the President's brother, a member of the regional Command of the Ba'th, the Commandant General of the Defence Brigades and, since March 1984, Vice-President of Syria, it is inevitable, even beneficial, for his country to accept the path of the Pax Americana in the Middle East. In Washington, in August 1982, and in Lausanne during the summer of 1984, he agreed to enter into contact with Israeli emissaries. Furthermore, he let Yasser Arafat know, during the Syrian–Palestinian battle for Tripoli in November 1983, that he supported his preference for a negotiated solution. According to his analysis, the Soviet alliance was above all a card that Damascus was keeping to trade dearly in negotiations with Washington and Jerusalem.

At the other extreme, other senior officers, such as General Ali Duba, the head of military intelligence, and General Ali Salih, the commander of the air force, wanted to enlarge the scope and strengthen the application of the Treaty of Cooperation with the USSR. Domestically, their position is approved by the supporters of the development of planning and tighter state control; the majority of these are newcomers on the political stage from peripheral rural areas, whereas the supporters of Rif'at al-Assad are rather drawn from the commercial bourgeoisie of Damascus, which is favourable to an economic opening to the West.

Between these two factions, which came to blows in the spring of 1984, President Assad tries to avoid deciding, and arbitrates slowly and with prudence, given the fact that the situation in the region harbours so many possibilities of evolution and that the local actors have the occasion to modify their analysis 'to suit their view'.

In the 'war of the camps' between the PLO and the Syrian sponsored Amal militia in Lebanon, the USSR has increasingly indicated support for Yasser Arafat's party. The Soviets are aware that should Hafez el-Assad manage to grab the Palestinian card, he would go further and faster along the road of direct negotiations with Israel, under American aegis. For the Syrians, Gorbachev's USSR is not just more dynamic and more attentive to the problems of the Middle East. It is also the great power which in the summer of 1986 promoted reconciliation between the various Palestinian factions, which openly encouraged the Lebanese Druze leader Walid Joumblatt to resist all foreign domination of his country, which protested in January 1987 against the massacre of the communists by Damascus' allies in Beirut, and, worst of all, which is about to reopen diplomatic relations with Israel. Realistically, General Assad knows he has to accommodate the USSR and did not send his troops into West Beirut in February 1987 before having sent his Chief of Staff, General Chehabi, to consult the Soviets. Above all, he has to keep the Soviet Union on his side until the international conference on the Middle East finally takes place.

From alliance to threat

For the Iraqi Ba'thists, the deterioration of the image of their Soviet ally occurred in the late 1970s. Up to a certain point, this deterioration arose from the suspicion and frustration felt by Saddam Hussein at developments in the regional and local situation.

First the regional situation: after 1978, the USSR was involved in one crisis after another, both in the Horn of Africa and in South-East Asia: Ethiopia–Somalia, Eritrea, Taraki's coup in Afghanistan, the change of government in People's Yemen, while the upheavals in Iran plunged its neighbours into uncertainty. Iraq feared becoming the 'Somalia of the Gulf' and seeing the Soviets invoke the defensive clauses of their treaty of alliance to intervene against the Ba'thist regime taking advantage of a communist 'bridgehead' inside,[47] so it stepped up its warnings to Moscow, closed its air space to Russian transport planes en route for Yemen and Ethiopia, and denounced a manoeuvre 'aimed at encircling the Gulf countries from Yemen, Ethiopia and Afghanistan'.[48] In the months that followed, rumours spread about a foiled pro-Soviet plot in Baghdad.[49] At the United Nations, where he was president of the General Assembly, and at the Islamic Conference in Islamabad [50] on 27–30 January 1980, the representative of the Ba'thist government delivered himself of condemnations of the Soviet intervention in Afghanistan, describing it as a 'serious, dangerous, inexcusable and unjustifiable mistake'.[51] In the eyes of the

Iraqi leaders, their Soviet ally had become an expansionist and dominating power 'trying to spread the ideology of Communism and increase its influence in world politics'.[52] Saddam Hussein then launched in the direction of the Arab states bordering the Gulf a proposal for a collective security pact,[53] in the spirit of non-alignment of which he saw himself the leader, and with the intention, soon disappointed, of bringing the oil sheikdoms together under his leadership.

The Ba'thists' mistrust of the Soviet Union developed when, immediately following the attack on Iran, Vice-President Tariq 'Aziz, who was sent to Moscow, had an Iraqi request for the supply of weapons turned down.[54] The sudden interruption of Soviet sales, which Baghdad probably expected, was denounced as pseudo-neutrality, incompatible with the 1972 treaty, and as *de facto* support for Khomeini's Iran to which the Soviet military was even suspected of leaking the plans of the 1980 Iraqi attack.[55] Soviet aid was only slowly resumed during 1981, because of the shift of the Iranian regime towards dictatorship but also because of the Iraqi army's change from being the aggressor to being on the defensive. The sale of spare parts, deliveries of arms, Mig-27s and an anti-aircraft defence network for the city of Baghdad[56] then took place on the realistic basis of 'mutually beneficial cooperation'.[57] In fact, in an interview given to the journal *Afrique–Asie* in July 1984, the same Tariq 'Aziz explained the row between the USSR and Iraq as due to the Kremlin's mistaken analysis of the nature of the Islamic revolution in Iran. To such analyses he contrasted the constancy of his own government, 'ever ready to relaunch relations'. Because the Soviet Union ended by appreciating its interest in the Gulf region, in the spring of 1984 Iraq received a supplier's credit for 'considerable quantities of sophisticated weaponry' amounting to almost two billion dollars, repayable over a long period; and because economic logic prevails in the USSR as elsewhere, new agricultural and oil cooperation agreements were signed between Baghdad and Moscow.

The deterioration in relations between the USSR and the Iraqi Ba'thists takes on an extra dimension when it is looked at from the angle of the domestic situation in Iraq, and in particular in the light of the conflict between the Ba'th and the ICP. Not only were the two parties separated by profound ideological differences between Arab nationalism, which is at the core of Ba'thist doctrine, and the communists' internationalism, but even more by their rivalry within the political system since, by extending its implantation among the Kurds and in the poor regions in the south with a Shi'ite majority, the ICP stood as the challenger to the Kassem regime right from 1958, and later to the Ba'thists.

During the first years of the regime (1968–74), this rivalry was deliberately concealed by the two allies who both assessed the benefits of their *entente*, with, moreover, the urgent encouragement of the USSR. In order to establish its legitimacy, the Ba'th thus benefited from civil peace, ensured also by the temporary quietening of the Kurdish revolt.[58] By 1976, however, [59] the communists were signalling a 'serious change' in relations between the two main members of the Front. The disagreement led to the arrest and imprisonment of thousands of ICP militants, and in May 1979, the execution of 39 leaders of the Party. After a long period of patience, the increasingly severe repression led the communists to break off relations with the regime in 1979[60] and take up the struggle.

At that time, the Ba'th Party prepared a list of the points of disagreement:[61] the ICP had criticized it for not applying the 1974 law on the autonomy of Kurdistan; since 1947, the communists had supported the right of Israel to exist and, even worse, today they maintained relations with the Israeli Rakah 'which is equivalent to the relations between Sadat and Begin'; they had publicly deplored the deterioration of relations between Syria and Iraq and blamed the Baghdad leaders for the break; they had approved the Soviet attitude in Eritrea and Somalia, towards Maoism, Eurocommunism, etc. The basic criticism related to the tactical participation of the ICP in the PNF, its masked intention to provoke an artificial cleavage between the 'progressives' and the 'conservatives' within the Ba'th and, ultimately, take over the Ba'thist revolution, all with the encouragement and help of the Soviet Union.

To understand the deterioration of the image of the Soviet Union among the Iraqi leaders and their disenchantment with the socialist 'model', it is not enough to point to the fears expressed as to Moscow's ambitions in the Middle East or duplicity by the communists within the PNF. It is true that after 1976 the USSR resumed its aid to the Kurdish movement and that in 1980 the Kurdish national parties, the KDP and the KPU, found themselves allied with the ICP in the opposition fronts[62] which waged the armed struggle against Saddam Hussein's regime. What must also be remembered are the limits put on the introduction into Iraq, as into Syria, of the model of the strong state backed by a single party posed by the specific political culture of the Arab East, the heir to both the segmentary system and Ottoman patrimonialism: in practice, agnatic, tribal and communal relations acted as a channel for relations between the state and the individual, taking precedence over party organizations which are often only empty shells, and family and local rivalries are fought out at the expense of state-building.

Furthermore, the origin of this deterioration and the breach between the progressive forces in Iraq and the Ba'th must be sought in the gradual transformation of that party from a nationalist and revolutionary party into a *nomenklatura* of functionaries; and above all in the appearance and development, around the state ruling group, taking advantage of the vast financial possibilities opened up to Iraq by its oil production after 1973, [63] of a new bourgeoisie which cornered the benefits of the agrarian reform, got rich in property and middleman activities and realized vast profits as the intermediary between the state sector and the numerous foreign private companies operating in the country.

In order to implement very ambitious development projects, this state bourgeoisie chose to reintegrate Iraq into a 'transnational' dependence.[64] It played down barter and aid relations with the USSR and the socialist states – which were never very important quantitatively – and went for an 'opening' to the states of Western Europe on an altogether different scale. In 1979, its main economic partners were West Germany, Japan, France and Italy. The appeal of Western goods, and in particular of the latest technology, which is costly and hard to maintain, was linked dialectically with the critique of Soviet aid, which was 'in any case ill-prepared and incapable of meeting all the development needs of the Arabs, even for those of them who are in a position to pay cash and in foreign exchange'.[65] At the same time, the middle and popular strata tended to lump together Soviet 'socialism' and the 'socialism' of Saddam Hussein's regime, with its administrative red-tape, its inequalities and above all the development of corruption.

In the 1970s, there was thus both a deterioration of the instrumental role of the USSR, since in the serious Arab–Israeli and Iraq–Iranian conflicts the alliance with Moscow did not deliver the goods expected by the two Ba'thist regimes, and the fragmentation of the state model in the eyes of leaders who turned to a mode of production depending on the West, whereas the Communist Party, decimated and virtually underground, was no longer in a position to disseminate a positive image of socialism.

What remains is the image of a superpower which it is worth accommodating and having as a partner, aside from all ideological considerations, even if the military and economic advantages conferred are limited. Along with the Irangate scandal in 1986, revealing that the US and Israel had restarted (if they had ever abandoned) arms sales to Iran, Baghdad also learnt that the US military were falsifying the information from the AWACS overflying Saudi Arabia. In these difficult times, Soviet support is once again indispensable and the image of the USSR as an ally re-emerges. But just as this rapprochement takes place, the Ba'athist government is taking spectacular measures to meet the cost of the war and the fall in oil prices. Denationalizations and government encouragements to businessmen and construction entrepreneurs mean that big capital is flourishing as never before in Iraq. Is this the post-war scenario already being sketched out? And what then will be the Soviet role in the reconstruction of Iraq?

When all is said and done, whether ally or threat, path to success or failure, the image of the USSR received and transmitted by the leaders of Syria and Iraq depends largely on the international context, according to whether it is a period of Soviet success or a period of roll-back, and whether the endemic crises in the Middle East are in an active stage or not, and the Arab regimes threatened. Paradoxical as it might appear, this image varies above all in the function of the domestic situation of each of the states we are looking at, the analysis made and the strategy adopted by its leaders. Thus the Soviet model becomes relevant in periods of political challenge threatening the legitimacy of the government, when pluralism is not enough to control the social ferment. It is upgraded to respond to shortages, even to economic crises, when the responses of the state bourgeoisie and the private traders aggravate the situation. The current difficulties of the Ba'thists might lead to a change of regime in both Syria and Iraq. And even if the ruling groups keep power, the image of the Soviet Union that they form and transmit will be modified, notwithstanding the nature of that state and the continuity of its strategy in the Middle East.

Notes

1. The Ba'thists took power in March 1962. In November 1970, General Assad ensured the triumph of the 'corrective' wing over the radical neo-Ba'thists of Salah Jdîd. See, E. Picard, 'La Syrie de 1946 à 1979', in A. Raymond, *La Syrie d'Aujourd'hui*, Paris, Editions du CNRS, 1980, pp. 168–84.

2. After an abortive attempt (February–November 1963), the Ba'th Party took power in Iraq in July 1968. M. Khadduri, *Socialist Iraq, A study in Iraqi politics since 1968*, Washington, Middle East Institute, 1978.

3. Alain Gresh, an expert on the Middle East, who agreed to read and comment on the first draft of this chapter, enriched its data base and discussed its analyses. I found the comments of the participants in the June 1983 seminar, those of Jean Leca, professor at the Institut d'Études Politiques de Paris, in particular, very useful when I came to rework the manuscript.

4. See M. Rodinson, *Marxisme et monde musulman*, Paris, Le Seuil, 1972, p. 434. (Eng. tr. by Michael Pallis, *Marxism and the Muslim World*, Zed Press, 1980).

5. Witness the revolt by Rashid 'Alî al-Qaylânî in Baghdad in 1941, in which volunteers from Syria took part. See H. Batatu, *The Old Social Classes and the Revolutionary Movements of Iraq. A study of Iraq's old landed and commercial classes and of its Communists, Ba'thists and Free Officers*, Princeton, Princeton University Press, 1978, p. 208.

6. See the lengthy discussion by M. Rodinson, op. cit., pp. 86 and 130–50.

7. See R. B. Betts, *Christians in the Arab East. A political study*, Athens, Lycabettus Press, 1975, p. 101.

8. The founder of the Arab Socialist Ba'th Party in 1943, Michel Aflak, was a Greek Orthodox from Damascus. In Iraq, the number three in the regime, the chief interlocutor with European governments, Târiq 'Azîz, is also a Christian.

9. See Kendal, 'Les Kurdes en Union Soviétique', in G. Chaliand (ed.), *Les Kurds et le Kurdistan*, Paris, Maspero, 1978, p. 323 (Eng. tr. M. Pallis, 'The Kurds in the Soviet Union', in *People without a Country, The Kurds and Kurdistan*, London, Zed Press, 1980, p. 220).

10. The best documented work on the subject is that by J. Couland, *Le Mouvement Syndical au Liban, 1919–1946*, Paris, Editions Sociales, 1970. Nothing comparable to H. Batatu's magisterial survey on Iraq exists for Syria.

11. The ICP was officially founded in 1934. See H. Batatu, op. cit., pp. 574 et seq.

12. On the birth and development of the labour movement in Syria see the unpublished thesis by E. Longuenesse, 'La classe ouvrière en Syrie, une classe en formation', Paris, EHESS, 1977, to which must be added a reading of J. Hannoyer and M. Seurat, *Etat et secteur public industriel en Syrie*, Beirut, Publications du CERMOC, 1979. For Iraq, see H. Batatu, op. cit., pp. 465–82.

13. See H. Batatu, op. cit., p. 584–5.

14. This is the central theme of Patrick Seale's work *The Struggle for Syria: a Study of Post-War Arab Politics, 1945–1958*, London, Oxford University Press, 1965. See also M. Rodinson, *Israël et le refus arabe*, Paris, Le Seuil, 1968, p. 81.

15. See E. F. Penrose, *Nations of the Modern World: Iraq*, London and Boulder, Westview Press, 1978, p. 122; and A. Dawisha, 'Introduction', in A. and K. Dawisha, *The Soviet Union in the Middle East*, London, Heinemann, 1982, p. 10.

16. M. Aflak, *Choix de textes de la pensée du fondateur du Parti Ba'th*, Madrid, Ba'th Socialist Party, 1977, p. 122 (In English as, Arab Ba'th Socialist Party, *Choice of Texts from the Ba'th Party Founder's Thought*, Baghdad (n.p.), 1977).

17. See H. Carrère d'Encausse, *La politique soviétique au Moyen-Orient*, Paris, Presses de la FNSP, pp. 168 et seq.

18. On its place in the Syrian economy, see M. Chatelus, 'La croissance économique: mutations des structures et dynamisme du déséquilibre', in A. Raymond, *La Syrie d'Aujourd'hui*, Paris, Editions du CNRS, 1980, pp. 235–36.

19. See the final part, devoted to the economy of the country, of E. F. Penrose, op. cit.

20. As G. Golan and I. Rabinovich point out in 'The Soviet Union and Syria: the limits of co-operation', in Y. Ro'i, *The Limits to Power: Soviet Policy in the Middle East*, London, Croom Helm, 1979, p. 220.

21. Long paeans of praise for the Soviet system attributed to the Syrian president's brother, R. al-Assad, the 'ideologue' of the regime, at the Seventh (Syrian) regional congress of the Ba'th Party (December 1979–January 1980) are reproduced by the opposition fortnightly of the Muslim Brothers of Syria, *al-Nadhîr*, no. 12, February 1980, pp. 18–20.

22. At the time of the entry of Syrian troops into Lebanon in 1976. Then at the time of the collapse of the PNF's common lists, before the legislative elections of 9–11 November 1981. And again after the Hama clashes in February 1982.

23. See A. Samarbakhsh, *Socialisme en Irak et en Syrie*, Paris, Anthropos, 1978, pp. 133–36.

24. In particular H. Carrère d'Encausse, op. cit. Also G. Golan, *Yom Kippur and After. The Soviet Union and the Middle East Crisis*, London, Cambridge University Press, 1977; A. and K. Dawisha, op. cit.; R. Khalidi, 'L'Union Soviétique et le Moyen-Orient', *Revue d'Etudes Palestiniennes*, no. 3, Spring 1982, pp. 91–104; and more recently A. Yodfat, *The Soviet Union and the Arabian Peninsula*, London, Croom Helm, 1983. Even F. Halliday, *Threat from the East? Soviet Policy from Afghanistan and Iran to the Horn of Africa*, rev. ed., Harmondsworth, Penguin, 1982), who distances himself from the thesis of a threat of destabilization by the Soviets in the Middle East in the 1970s, does not free himself entirely of this perspective.

25. The detailed chronology of the Iraqi–Soviet agreements is given by the *Fiches du Monde arabe* (Beirut), no. 2,095, 2,100, 2,101, 2,107, 2,110 and 2,115. For Syria see the *Fiches* no. 1,132, 1,138, 1,144, 1,150, 1,156 and 1,743.

26. *Al-Thawra* (daily, Baghdad), 12 April 1972.

27. Article 7 of the treaty.

28. 4 August 1970, 10 February 1972, 21 March and 10 October 1973, 31 January 1977 and 11 December 1978.

29. According to the *Fiches du Monde arabe*, Assad went to Moscow on 1 February 1971 (his first visit abroad as head of state) and 5 July 1972, 3 May 1973, 9 October 1975, 20 February and 5 October 1978, 17 October 1979 and 8 October 1980.

30. Alexei Kosygin, Soviet Prime Minister, was on an official visit to Damascus on 1 June 1976, the day Syrian troops in Lebanon attacked the left and the Palestinians. On 11 July, Leonid Brezhnev sent Assad a strong note urging him to put an end to the fighting and in August the USSR suspended all military supplies to Syria, which it only resumed in the spring of 1977, following the reconciliation between the Syrian government and the PLO. For the Soviet position in the Syrian–Palestinian crisis, see 'Find a way out of the Lebanese impasse', *Pravda*, 8 September 1976, translated into French and published in *Maghreb-Machrek*, 74, October–November–December 1976, p. 78–80.

31. At the Khartoum summit (1967) the oil states committed themselves to supplying it, as part of the war effort, with $500 million a year; one billion at the Algiers summit (1973) and then 2.1 billion at the Baghdad summit (1978). The actual outlays, tied to the regional political conjuncture, are irregular.

32. Syria lost five Migs in September and October 1979. See E. Picard, 'Les militaires syriens devant les accords de Camp David', *Défense nationale*, August–September 1981, pp. 35–51.

33. Ahmad Iskandar Ahmad in *Mostaqbal* (Paris), 2 September 1980.

34. Ibid.

35. The installation of three batteries of SA-6 and two SA-3 missiles in the Beqaa valley on 28 April 1981 forced the Israeli air force to break off its support for the Phalangists who had to leave Zahlé. See E. Picard, 'Libanon in der Existenzkrise, Strategien nach Camp David', *Europa Archiv*, January 1982, pp. 39–48.

36. On the revelations about these bases by Jerusalem at the beginning of January 1983, the confirmation by Washington and then by Moscow in February, but never officially by Damascus, see the chronology in *Maghreb-Machrek*, no. 100, April–May–June 1983, p. 73.

37. Najah al-Attâr, Minister of Culture, to the semi-official daily *Tishrin*, 28 March 1983: 'The USSR will take a direct part in the fighting alongside Damascus in the event of an Israeli attack. It will not be satisfied with strengthening Syria's defensive capacities but it will stand alongside it militarily'.

38. On 9 June, all the SA-2 and SA-6 missiles were destroyed; in six days, Syria lost almost 80 Migs, it suffered '4,500 dead including 80 pilots' (Y. Shakkour, Syrian Ambassador in France, in Paris, 31 May 1983).

39. Interview with General Assad in *Nahâr al-'Arabî al-Duwalî* (Paris), 30 October 1982: 'We sometimes experience the lack of certain types of weapons, that in no way diminishes the position of the Soviets alongside us in our just fight, nor the continuing support of the Soviets in arms and in international bodies.'

40. See for example the article by D. Middleton in the *New York Times* 19 September 1982, 'Soviet weapons outclassed in Lebanon. How Israel decimated the tanks and mobile missiles delivered to Syria'.

41. The speech is reproduced in *al-Ba'th*, a Syrian daily, of 21 November 1982.

42. See F. Halliday, op. cit., p. 63; and A. Samarbakhsh, op. cit., p. 134.

43. Syria accepted Security Council resolutions 338 and, consequently, 242 at the time of the negotiation of the Syrian–Israeli disengagement agreement of May 1974, when the relations of force seemed re-established in favour of the Arabs. After 1976, it was again expressing its reservations.

44. On the position of the USSR in 1976–77, see note 30 above.

45. The aggravation of the conflict in June 1983, between the Syrian regime and Yasser Arafat at the head of the PLO reveals the extreme difficulty, or even the powerlessness of the Soviet Union to arbitrate between its two allies in the Middle East, which could both easily abandon their Soviet partner and enter into the process of the 'Pax Americana'.

46. A single example: at the beginning of June 1983, the American Defense Department sent information on the armed positions in the Beqaa valley, gathered by satellite, 'to the Israelis and the Syrians'. See also R. Khalidi, op. cit., p. 191.

47. In an interview with *Le Monde* of 9 January 1971, Saddam Hussein accused the Iraqi Communist leaders of 'confusing their interests with those of the external enemies' of which, in his opinion, they constituted the 'bridgehead'.

48. Ministry of Culture and Information (Baghdad): 'What are the results that the Soviet Union and the World are waiting for after the intervention in Afghanistan?', 1980, p. 28.

49. *Al-Nahâr al-'Arabî al-Duwalî* (Paris), 20 May and 3 June 1978. See also A. and L. Chabry, 'L'Irak et l'émergence de nouveaux rapports politiques inter-arabes', *Maghreb-Machrek*, 88, April–May–June 1980, pp. 5–25.

50. R. Santucci, 'La solidarité islamique à l'épreuve de l'Afghanistan', *Revue Française de Science Politique*, vol. 32, no. 3, June 1982 (the crises in Cambodia and Afghanistan seen from Asia), p. 500. Syria, which boycotted the meeting, reiterated

on 20 February its 'rejection of any military intervention in the affairs of small states by the great powers' (interview with Prime Minister R. Al-Kasm in the Lebanese weekly *al-Sayyâd*).

51. S. Hammadi, Minister of Foreign Affairs to *Newsweek*, 25 February 1980, p. 56.

52. Ibid.

53. 8 February 1980. Text in *Maghreb-Machrek*, no 88, April–May–June 1980, pp. 89–91.

54. 22 September 1980. See interview with Târiq 'Azîz with *Le Monde*, 20 December 1980.

55. Yet another sign of the 'Somali syndrome' among the Iraqi Ba'thists. The information, given by an Italian journalist, was repeated by Eric Rouleau in *Le Monde*, 6 January 1981.

56. *Al-Charq al Awsat* (London), 28 June 1981.

57. *Pravda* of 11 April 1981, quoted by A. Yodfat, op. cit., p. 159 note 34.

58. H. Batatu, op. cit., p. 1100 and I. Vanly, 'Le Kurdistan d'Iraq', in G. Chaliand, op. cit., p. 249.

59. The political report of the Central Committee of the ICP dated 10 March 1978 says 'for two years'.

60. The ICP's participation in the government and the PNF is attested up to the autumn of 1979. See notably *Le Monde*, 6 April 1979. In December 1978, the Arab communist and labour parties meeting in Damascus issued a protest against the anti-communist repression in Iraq. An article entitled 'Stop the Repressions and Persecutions' by a leader of the party, N. Duleimi, criticizing the Ba'thist government, was published in the *World Marxist Review* in March 1979.

61. In a letter to the members of the provincial committees of the ICP dated September 1978.

62. The National Democratic Front and the Democratic Patriotic Front. See P. Ribau in *Révolution*, 107, 19 March 1982.

63. On the perverse effects of the oil rent on the Iraqi economy see M. Farouk-Sluglett and P. Sluglett, *Iraq since 1958*, London, KPI, 1987, pp. 239–254. Also M. Ja'far, 'Les limites de l'industrialisation du monde arabe: étude de cas de l'Irak', *Khamsin*, 4, 1977, pp. 88–104.

64. This is the formula used by Samir Amin in the harsh conclusion of his work *Irak et Syrie*, Paris, Editions de Minuit, 1982, p. 144.

65. Ministry of Culture and Information, Baghdad, op. cit., p. 21.

3 Turkey between its Western Patron and the 'Big Neighbour to the North'

Semih Vaner

A study of the Turkish perception of the USSR, and also of Russia, which it is difficult to dissociate from it, would require a number of volumes. As heir to the Ottoman Empire which had, over the centuries, conflict-laden relations with Tsarist Russia, as a state bordering on the USSR and as a member of the Atlantic alliance, Turkey occupies a special place in the Third World. In addition to these constraints of a historical and geographical nature, there is a series of ideological, cultural, religious and ethnic features that have contributed to shaping Turkish–Soviet relations. Without totally ignoring these very important features, we shall concentrate on a factor that seems just as important as the mistrust traditionally aroused by the 'Big Neighbour to the North'.

This is the geostrategic context and the perception of it by political actors and decision-makers in Turkey. The attitude of the USSR, also influenced by this factor, resulted in Turkey abandoning its policy of neutrality and committing itself firmly to the Western camp, following the Second World War. This commitment in turn had an effect on the East–West confrontation in which the Cuban missile crisis was one of the most dramatic incidents in which, yet again, Turkey served as a bargaining counter between the two great powers. We shall include in this diplomatic perspective an analysis of the position of the USSR in the disputes between the two countries bordering the Aegean Sea (Greece and Turkey) and the economic aspect which has assumed considerable importance in Turkish–Soviet relations in the last two decades.

Historical, ideological and cultural background

In the time of the Ottoman Empire, as in the time of Republican Turkey, the 'Russian' and later Soviet element has constituted a constant element in the forefront of Turkish foreign policy.[1] In the host of historical studies that appeared during the years of the Cold War, reference was repeatedly made to the 'thirteen wars' between the two 'centuries-old enemies', one controlling access to the Mediterranean, the other considering that to be deprived of this access was unacceptable. It is extremely easy to find references to these preoccupations in the speeches of Russian and Soviet leaders. Thus the Foreign Minister in the short-lived Kerensky government, Miliukov, had no hesitation in declaring to the Duma: 'We shall not end the war without securing an outlet to the open sea. The annexation of the Straits will not be a territorial annexation, for vast Russia has no need of new territories but she cannot prosper without access to the open sea.'[2] More than the other twelve, this war, ended by the October Revolution, left indelible traces. In the territories in the east subjected to Russian occupation, the atrocious memories of the sufferings endured by Turkish soldiers who perished in their tens of thousands, more from epidemics, the cold, and undernourishment than from the fighting, remain very much alive. To say this is to say how much the recurrent feelings of fear and hostility towards the 'hereditary enemy', profoundly rooted in the popular consciousness and fuelled by a visceral anti-communism, are certainly not unconnected with Turkey's total commitment to the West over the last 40 years.

Yet, the links that were established at the time of the Turkish war of independence between the two defeated powers in the First World War were so cordial that they caused concern in Western capitals. The two 'natural allies' saw mutual advantages in this collaboration. The Bolshevik leaders found in the Anatolian resistance a support against the British, notably on the Transcaucasian front. Mustafa Kemal, who had made the alliance with the Soviet Republic one of the main planks of his strategy, had less room for manoeuvre: he had to win the confidence of the Bolsheviks without attracting the hostility of the Great Powers, and the Bolsheviks, on certain points, such as the territories claimed by Armenia, remained 'untreatable'.[3] He had obtained from the Soviet Union, despite its enormous privations, valuable economic aid.

The cooperation agreement of 1921 was followed by the Treaty of Friendship and Neutrality of 17 December 1925 by which Turkey and the USSR agreed to abstain from any aggression against each other, to remain neutral in the event of aggression by a third party and not to enter any political alliance or agreement directed against the other. Despite this treaty, relations between Ankara and Moscow were rather distant without being hostile, until 1929, when they improved with the signing of a new treaty, which agreed that the conclusion by one of the respective governments of a political agreement with a third state having a common land or sea border with the other party, would be subject to the consent of that party.

After 1936, Turkish diplomacy effected a rapprochement with Britain and France, which resulted in the treaty of alliance between the three countries, signed on 19 October 1939. 'In short', René Massigli, then French Ambassador in Ankara, would later write, 'it was enough for the leaders in Ankara to have lashed the Turkish galliot to the Franco-British man-of-war to retain vis-à-vis their neighbours the freedom of action that would enable them to face up to the great variety of situations they were likely to encounter.'[4] The Turkish refusal to enter the war was principally dictated by mistrust of the USSR whose diplomacy and propaganda after 1939 manifested some signs of hostility towards Turkey.

During the whole of this single-party period in which Kemalism was erected into the official ideology of the Turkish state, communist activities were severely repressed. Mustafa Kemal set the tone as early as 1920, in a letter addressed to the commander of the western front, Ali Fuad Pasha: 'The establishment of a communist organization inside the country is totally against our interests since *anyone who says communist organization says complete submission to Russia . . .* Of course, communism and bolshevism must not be opposed openly.'[5] More than for doctrinal reasons, the propagation of communism and bolshevism in Turkey had to be prevented, in order to ward off Soviet interference in the affairs of Anatolia. This identification of communist propaganda with Soviet penetration was to be a constant feature of Kemalist ideology. It would mark the elites of the post-Kemalist period and constitute one of the major obstacles to the formation and progress of left-wing parties.

Conscious, however, of how important a communist party could be in forming a friendship with Moscow that he deemed to be essential for Turkey,[6] Mustafa Kemal had not, initially, judged it opportune to oppose the creation of one. In the years 1920–21, in the midst of the national liberation war, organizations such as the Green Army (*Yesil ordu*) the Popular Group (*Halk zümres*) which succeeded it and the Popular Communist Party THIF (*Türkiye halk istirakiyyûn firkasi*)[7] without any real audience among the masses nor ideological rigour, proclaimed a mishmash of bolshevism, pan-Asianism and Islam, except for the THIF which, staying close to Kemalist principles, stressed the separation of state and religion.[8] These organizations had an ephemeral existence as did the 'official' Turkish Communist Party created out of nothing by Mustafa Kemal and led by his own Minister of Finance. The obvious purpose of this initiative, whose 'fallacious' character Moscow rapidly exposed, through the International, was to pinpoint 'subversive' elements and give tokens of goodwill to the Soviet Union.

Only the Turkish Communist Party (*Türkiye Komünist Partisi*),[9] created in Baku in March 1920, succeeded in being different from the others. Initially infiltrated by Unionist figures who used it to create a platform to oppose Mustafa Kemal, then dominated by Mustafa Suphi who gradually got rid of these latter elements, and finally torn between the need to sustain the anti-imperialist struggle and the need to establish itself firmly in the country, the TKP had an extremely difficult, even dramatic, existence after the murder of its leaders. Forced underground and operating from abroad, the TKP was later wholly under Moscow's thumb. At the same time, the Turkish Labour Party (*Türkiye Isçi Partisi*), legal except during the military interludes, purged of is 'revisionist' elements after the events in Czechoslovakia but very much weakened (3% of the votes in 1965, only 0.1% in 1977) did not conceal its pro-Sovietism, while at the same time endeavouring to propagate the image of a party concerned with its autonomy and denouncing Turkey's craven subordination to the Western bloc. Finally, the Turkish Workers and Peasants Party (*Türkiye Isçi Köylü Partisi*), following a pro-Chinese line, legal before the 1980 military coup, but with no representation in parliament, conversely went so far as to call for the closing of the Straits to Soviet vessels.

Most Kurdish organizations claiming to be Marxist such as (*Özgürlük yolu*) ('The road to freedom'), *Roja Walat* ('The sun of the country'), the DDKD (Revolutionary Democratic Cultural Association) and the PKK (Kurdistan Workers Party) all dismantled by the military junta in late 1980, claimed to be resolutely pro-Soviet and sought Moscow's support in their struggle, but Moscow remained carefully prudent and did not encourage separatism. Two other left-wing Kurdish organizations have remained severely critical of the USSR: *Kawa*, pro-Chinese, more or less put the struggle against the USSR and the struggle for the independence of Kurdistan on virtually the same level, while *Rizgari* criticized the CPSU for never having made a statement on the right of Kurds to self-determination.[10]

As the historian P. Dumont points out, in most Turkish 'communist' organizations, in the early 1920s, there was an obvious tendency to pan-Asianism or even pan-Turkism. The most peculiar example of these pan-Turkists and pan-Turanians[11] was surely that of Enver, Minister of War in 1914 and the main person responsible for the Ottoman Empire's entry into the war on Germany's side. Exiled to the Soviet Union, Enver, with his Unionist supporters, first gave, 'give or take a few reservations and some ideological fudging, his support to the bolshevik cause'[12]; he died in August 1922, at the head of the Bismachis, during an expedition to Turkestan, against the Red Army. Without openly disowning this undertaking, doomed as it was from the outset to failure, Mustafa Kemal did not condemn it so as to retain a means of pressure against Moscow. But, at the same time, he took good care not to give it his blessing, so as not to attract Soviet Russia's hostility and also so as to deny support to a potential and determined political opponent.

The presence in the Soviet Union of Turkish ethnic groups such as the Uzbeks – which, with a total of some 14 million, constitute the second largest Turkish group in the world after the Turks in Turkey – the Kazakhs, the Tatars and the Azeris to mention only the largest ones,[13] numbering tens of millions, had a major, though latent, impact on Turkish–Soviet relations. Since the end of the Second World War, however, Turkey has refrained from exercising cultural and political influence on these groups or exploiting this situation for foreign policy ends. In the 1940s, financed by the nazis who were seeking to drag Turkey into the war against the USSR, the pan-Turanian movement had experienced a certain revival, but it was soon checked. More recently, backed by a section of the youth facing an identity crisis, Colonel Türkes' National Action Party (6.4% of the votes in the 1977 elections) has been the main political force making pan-Turanianism a plank in its political struggle. It is easy to see the impact that the presence of Turkish ethnic groups in the USSR would have, were a right-wing nationalist government tempted to exploit it even to come to power in Turkey, especially if it is remembered that these groups have a birth rate three times higher than that of the Slav populations.

Turkey in the American 'containment' policy

Clientelism, a concept often used in internal studies, could also be used in international relations. It may for example be thought that clientelism is one of the forms, one of the mechanisms of international domination.[14] In the relationship between a patron-state and a client-state, all the features of clientelism are to be found, i.e. the relationship of reciprocity (or exchange), the relationship of dependence, and the vertical structure, all except the interpersonal dimension.

Following the Second World War, all the conditions seemed to exist for the voluntary entry of Turkey into a clientelist relationship with the West, and, more particularly, with the United States. In fact, the 'modernization' of Turkey had, since the 19th Century, been posed in terms of Westernization. Moreover, this option was confirmed authoritatively and irreversibly by Mustafa Kemal and his successors. In addition, there was the necessity to have recourse to foreign aid to promote the take-off of a lifeless economy. The rising Turkish commercial bourgeoisie was then demanding closer links with the capitalist world. There was also a need to find the means to finance a powerful army on permanent alert and to do so despite a declared neutrality. But only the West could meet Turkey's needs, even though the Marshall Plan had, for example, only a limited impact on the Turkish economy. Added to these economic imperatives was the quest for security guarantees, to counter ill-received Soviet pressures. At first, between 1946 and 1963, and more particularly between 1950 and 1960, when Menderes' resolutely Atlanticist Democratic Party was in power, this clientelist relationship[15] took the form of a dependence that was close, not to say over-zealous or servile.[16] After 1964, Turkey attempted to loosen this excessive dependence through an anti-clientelist strategy. Conscious of the geostrategic advantages it possessed (the fact that it borders on the USSR) Ankara endeavoured with varying success to obtain the maximum possible economic and military aid both from the West and the USSR.

'One had to be a Turk, with his hereditary infallible flair for sniffing out the complicated detours of the Slav mentality, with his national instinct for the Russian threat, his sure intuition of how to deal with this danger and his acute security consciousness, in order to adapt as required to the changing demands of the situation',[17] wrote F. C. Erkin, the Director-General of Political Affairs at the Ministry of Foreign Affairs in 1939, after criticizing the British for not being able to understand the 'underlying reasons' for the Soviet demands made in the late 1930s.

During a visit to Moscow, in September 1939, Saraçoğlu, the Turkish Minister of Foreign Affairs, had refused to study and discuss Molotov's demand for the alteration of certain articles in the Montreux Convention.[18] The Turkish leaders' anxiety was deepened by the conciliatory attitude adopted by both Churchill and Roosevelt towards Stalin. In Teheran, in November 1943, then in Moscow in October 1944, Stalin had in fact raised the question of 'warm water' and claimed that Turkey could 'grip Russian trade by the throat'.[19]

On 20 March 1945, the USSR abrogated the Treaty of Neutrality and Friendship signed with Turkey in 1925. It informed the Turkish government on 7 June of the same year that, in order to obtain a similar agreement, Turkey should hand back the territories of Kars and Ardahan, annexed by Russia in 1878 and restored to Turkey in 1921, and accept the revision of the Montreux Convention so that the security of the Straits would be assured jointly by Turkey and the USSR. Finally, it demanded the establishment of a Soviet military base in the Dardanelles.[20] Even if it is somewhat exaggerated to say of the Turks' reaction that 'the hatred of communism was only equalled by the admirable élan of patriotism and resolve that had gripped the whole nation',[21] Stalin's demands unquestionably caused sharp concern and a profound unease in Turkish governing circles and public opinion. By thus provoking a crisis with unforeseeable consequences, the Soviets exacerbated the feeling of those in Turkey who felt that the question of the Straits was simply a façade behind which the Soviets were, in fact, hoping to change the regime in Turkey, and to put in charge of the country leaders ready to play the role of 'friends of the USSR', a role already played by others in countries that were in varying degrees satellites.[22] While the Soviet threat was indeed real, it seems reasonably certain that it also provided an excellent opportunity for the anti-Soviets and anti-communists to stoke up – and do so for decades – the traditional feelings of fear of the 'Russian danger' and 'hatred' of communism.

With a 'stable state and an army capable of holding up an attacking force for long enough for intervention by the Western powers',[23] Turkey, like Iran, manifested a determination to resist by categorically rejecting the Soviet demands while reiterating its readiness to negotiate another treaty taking account of the new conditions that existed. It sought external support which was not long in coming. Churchill and Truman overrode Turkey's opposition to its dispute with the USSR being discussed at Potsdam where the two Western statesmen used conciliatory language to Stalin who repeated his demand for Soviet–Turkish co-responsibility over the Straits. Basing themselves on these facts, several Turkish intellectuals who have not received the hearing they deserve and who are not necessarily pro-Soviet, were later to dispute the view that the United States had 'saved' Turkey:[24] the Truman doctrine, they stressed, was only proclaimed at a date when the Soviet threat had ceased to exist.

Apart from the reasons already mentioned, the only result of the Soviet attempts between 1945 and 1947 to modify the status quo with Turkey was that Ankara abandoned the policy of neutrality which it had practised continuously since the birth of the Republic and was forced actively to seek an alliance with the United States. Acceptance of the Truman doctrine formulated in 1947 and intended 'to support free peoples who are resisting attempted subjugation by armed minorities or by outside pressures', the despatch of an expeditionary force to Korea, and joining the Atlantic Pact in 1952 gave concrete expression to this option. When in 1949, the Turkish request to join the Atlantic Pact met with opposition from several Western governments who did not want to extend the area covered by the treaty, claiming that the Soviet Union must not be given the impression that it was being encircled, N. Sadak, the Turkish Minister of Foreign Affairs, stated: 'If it is a matter of opposing the red peril, nowhere is the threat so direct and so close as that which the Kremlin holds over Istanbul and the Straits. Could it be that, precisely, some of the states parties to the pact feel that the situation of Turkey is too exposed to undertake commitments towards it?'[25]

The Turkish leaders saw only 'a change of tactics rather than a change of strategy'[26] when on 30 May 1953, that is less than three months after the death of Stalin, Moscow addressed a note to Ankara, stating that 'the governments of the SSRs of Armenia and Georgia have deemed it possible to renounce their territorial demands on Turkey'.[27] Moscow's 'peace offensive' ran up against the intense suspicion of Menderes' Democratic Party. In a statement to the foreign press, Menderes clearly expressed the state of mind of Turkish leaders towards both the USSR and the neutralist movement: 'Until today, examples have shown us that the principle of "peaceful coexistence", proposed by Russia, does not take the form of peace and understanding . . . but is translated into the submission of the attacked state before the domination of one country by another. We must then choose between submission, that is disappearance, and resolving to defend ourselves. Neutralism is not a third way possible for us.'[28]

During the 1950s, Turkish diplomacy repeatedly offered its services to help the Western powers create military pacts in the Middle East designed to contain the Soviet Union. Despite the failure – because of Egypt's hostility – of the attempt in the early 1950s, to set up a Middle East 'defence' pact, put forward as an extension of the Atlantic Pact, new attempts directed at the same goal were made following Eisenhower's appointment of John Foster Dulles as US Secretary of State. Between Turkey, a member of NATO, and Pakistan, a member of SEATO, there was a gap which Dulles endeavoured to fill by encouraging the creation of an anti-Soviet alliance among the countries of the Middle East.[29] The Baghdad Pact – which later became CENTO – signed in 1955 between Turkey and Iraq, and which Great Britain, Pakistan and Iran joined one after the other, reflected this same determination. The Eisenhower doctrine of 1957, a new version for the Middle East of the Truman doctrine, justified in advance the principle of military intervention by the United States in the Middle East in the event 'of direct or indirect aggression by international communism'. It also received the backing of Menderes, anxious to give proof of goodwill to the United States whose financial assistance was increasingly vital to him. Confronted with an economic crisis and considerable external indebtedness, Menderes did put out feelers to the Soviet Union, but this attempt failed because of the 1960 *coup d'état;* some feel that this coup was motivated by the need to put a stop to this opening to the East.

Turkey's alignment with the Western camp throughout this period was so total and its distancing from its Arab–Muslim environment so exaggerated that one analyst of Turkish foreign policy has detected in it the continuity of a certain 'strategy aiming at regional hegemony', even a 'sub-imperialism'.[30] Such an interpretation is not altogether wrong, especially if one remembers the regret expressed among an important fringe of the ruling class, even of society, for having 'ceded' Mosul and Kirkuk, regrets often tinged with the unadmitted desire to get them back. Just as it would, however, be rather excessive to overestimate, for example, the pressure exerted on Bulgaria for it to agree to a modification of the border before World War II, so it would be excessive to lend credence to the idea of any simple overlap between pan-Turanian demands and Ankara's diplomacy during the Second World War.[31] In our opinion, these pressures and demands had to do more with diplomatic tactics than with a fixed design by Turkish leaders often constrained to play a double game and to seek means of countering the contradictory pressures put on them by Berlin and Moscow. It would consequently be difficult to conclude that a strategy aiming at hegemony 'presided over'[32] Turkish diplomacy, during or after the war, even though aims of this sort were not absent at some moments and in the minds of some politicians (it is enough to think of more recent statements by Erbakan and Türkeş about Cyprus or the Aegean islands).

The turning-point of 1963–64: towards a normalization of relations with Moscow

Admiral P. Célérier cites Turkey as an example of a 'poor country with little intrinsic value' but which has been able to 'achieve political power through skilfully exploiting the advantages of its position'.[33] In the conditions prevailing in the 1950s, Turkey played an essential role in the US strategy of containment (use of its aerodromes by bombers loaded with potential 'massive reprisals', intermediate range missile bases).[34] At the beginning of the 1960s, it lost some of its strategic importance as a result of the withdrawal of missiles from its territory and, above all, the Soviet advance in the Middle East and the eastern Mediterranean. This last factor, combined with the international climate of détente, was not unconnected with the Turkish–Soviet rapprochement which began in 1963–64. But the decisive role in this was played by the December 1963 Cyprus crisis. President Johnson's letter, which informed the then Prime Minister, Ismet Inönü, that the NATO weapons Washington had delivered could not be used without its agreement, especially if the conflict threatened to involve two members of the Atlantic Alliance, provoked an unprecedented wave of anti-Americanism in Turkey and, as a corollary, a rapprochement with the USSR.[35] Despite Demirel's militant anti-communism and the fact that he could not in the least be suspected of pro-Sovietism, his Justice Party government, which ruled alone from 1965 to 1971, worked towards cooperation with Moscow which was pursued throughout the 1970s.

It is important to stress here that the shift in Turkish external policy occurred in a specific context linked to social and intellectual changes in Turkish society. The section of public opinion feeling itself concerned by foreign policy was growing larger and larger. It was going beyond the limited circles previously considered (press, ruling groups), and spreading to other strata of the population, particularly the intelligentsia and student youth. 1968 saw the emergence of a very lively debate among groups holding opposing opinions on foreign policy and its economic, financial and social implications. The stakes appeared serious and important; almost invariably negative assessments were made of the 1940–60 period.[36] This period, which coincided with the end of 'bipartisan' foreign policy,[37] saw organizations like the Turkish Labour Party and, after 1967, the Confederation of Reformist Trade Unions (DISK) attempt, with a section of the left-wing press, and with some success, to change the USSR's unfavourable image in Turkey.

A further step was taken towards a rapprochement by Bülent Ecevit, the leader of the Republican People's Party. On his visit to Moscow in June 1978, he let it be understood that Turkey was proposing to reduce its cooperation with the United States and its participation in NATO and that this step was dictated by 'the awareness that the threat weighing on its security did not come from the USSR or the other socialist countries'.[38] The path travelled in 20 years was considerable, even though the document signed by the Turkish Prime Minister at the end of his visit to the Soviet Union did not go as far as the 1971 political agreement between Moscow and Bonn.[39] Ankara's Soviet policy was part of the Ecevit government's new 'national security concept' (*ulusal güvenlik kavramı*), a concept which was however, insufficiently defined and difficult to apply because of the internal political and economic conjuncture and the shortness of the periods in government of the Republican People's Party.

The review of Turkish foreign policy in the 1960s also led to an opening to the countries of the Middle East. In 1967, in its desire to improve its relations with the Arab countries, Turkey granted oil refuelling facilities to Iraqi Migs going to the Soviet Union for maintenance, a move which was contrary to Turkey's commitments within NATO.[40]

More recently, the changes that have occurred in this same region (fall of the Iranian monarchy, Soviet invasion of Afghanistan and the Iraq–Iran war), which coincided with the military's taking power in Turkey, have again brought out the geostrategic importance of the country. The Reagan administration considers Turkey as one of the key elements of its strategy for containing the Soviet drive in the Middle East. In fact, since 1980, American and NATO leaders have repeatedly made statements suggesting that pressure would be put on Turkey[41] to commit itself unequivocally to the defence of Western interests in the Middle East.

Turkey, being anxious not to poison its relations with either the Soviet Union or its southern neighbours, initially refused to accept an active role in the various Western scenarios. Thus, during a visit by Caspar Weinberger to Ankara, in December 1981, the possible contribution of Turkey to the Rapid Deployment Force was not officially raised. The Turks who feel – as indeed do the Gulf countries themselves – that the defence of the region is their affair only, had indicated that they did not want to serve as the spearhead of American troops in the Middle East, whether by granting them stockpiling facilities or allowing them the use of military bases. There are, however, grounds for wondering about Turkey's capacity to resist, especially given the state of its economy, which is heavily dependent on American aid, and the presence in the corridors of power of groups pushing for a greater commitment alongside the United States.

Even though the United States has not made any official proposal for the establishment of an RDF base, the recent conclusion of a memorandum of understanding between the two countries on the modernization of the bases at Erzurum and Batman and the building of aerodromes in eastern Turkey (Mus) is such as to confirm the influence of this 'pro-American' tendency. It may be wondered, indeed, how far Turkey would be able to refuse its contribution in the event of an open crisis in the region. It is still the case that the question of the RDF disturbs public opinion. Moreover, many Turks wonder whether a crisis in the region might not suit the great powers. The Soviets would find a pretext to move to action, while the Americans would take advantage of it to increase their military build-up. At the end of the day, the only sufferers would be the Turks, who, in any hypothesis, would see themselves constrained to become, at their expense and for others' benefit, the region's policemen.

The USSR 'seen' and 'heard' from Turkey

The position of Turkey, which possesses ultra-modern monitoring posts, was strengthened after the departure of the Shah and the 'loss' of American monitoring posts in Iran. Three stations provide America round the clock with some 25% of the information concerning Soviet strategic missile tests: Belbasi, not far from Ankara, where seismologists detect Soviet underground nuclear explosions: Pirinçlik, in eastern Anatolia, where two radar stations follow satellite movements; Sinop, on the Black Sea, a centre for collecting electronic intelligence, and detecting troop movements in the USSR. These posts belong to the American Central Intelligence Agency, responsible for all matters to do with deciphering, decoding, jamming and detecting communications.

All the American agency's monitoring posts play a role in monitoring the Soviet test centres as Kapustinyar, east of Volgograd, and Tyuratam, near the Aral Sea. This last site tests Soviet SS-18 and SS-19 intercontinental missiles, and, more particularly, the independently targeted multiple warheads. These posts are also responsible for intercepting communications between different units, public bodies, and so on, inside the Soviet Union. In addition to these monitoring posts, Turkey is home to 14 air surveillance and alert stations of the NADGE network and eleven posts in NATO's ACE HIGH network. Furthermore, on the shores of the Sea of Marmara, the Karamürsel post makes it possible to identify every ship and submarine passing through the Straits, and determine their type of armament and the number of missiles they are carrying, while at the base at Incirlik nuclear-headed missiles are based.

The monitoring posts, as well as the strategic ballistic missile launching bases, were established on Turkish territory by virtue of bilateral agreements concluded with the United States in the 1950s. It was from one of these bases, at Incirlik, that, in late April 1960, a U-2 military plane took off which, after a stopover at Peshawar in Pakistan, crossed the Soviet border and penetrated over 2,000 km inside the USSR before being brought down. The confusion of the Turkish response to the Soviet note which declared 'that by placing its territory at the disposal of the United States for the establishment of air bases and the carrying out by American planes of aggressive acts against the Soviet Union [the Turkish government] makes itself an accomplice in such acts and, hence, assumes a heavy responsibility for any possible consequences brought about by these acts',[42] eloquently reflected the embarrassment of the leaders in Ankara. After banning overflights by U-2s after 1967, Turkey asked the Americans for a review of the treaty – which had been initiated by the Democratic government and signed shortly after the military came to power in 1960 – whose terms (meteorological and scientific observations) were simply a camouflage for military surveillance. On the basis of Soviet protests, it called on the members of NATO for increased 'security' norms for the country in exchange for the continuation of U-2 operations. After 1979, when the issue of the verification of Soviet compliance with the SALT II agreements was being discussed and despite urgent requests by Washington, Ecevit, caught up in a host of economic difficulties, but supported by the opposition and the general staff on this issue, made the at least tacit consent of Moscow (which did not give it) a prerequisite to the authorization of overflights by U-2 reconnaissance planes.[43]

The October 1962 Cuban missile crisis was as serious as the U-2 affair: it showed how much Turkey was within the scope of what Pentagon strategists call 'small-scale adventurism'[44] and revealed that the country risked at any moment becoming an area where the two great powers might try out their conventional weapons. Nikita Khrushchev offered to withdraw the missiles that he had sent to Cuba in exchange for a renunciation by the United States of their bases in Turkey, threateningly suggesting that he was 'able to guarantee the integrity of Turkey only if the United States guarantees, before the UN, the integrity of Cuba'.[45] Turkey, the only country in the West, except Italy, to have agreed to the installation of Jupiters on its territory, resigned itself, unwillingly, to the dismantling of these missiles, Kennedy having decided to 'convince' the Turks 'to ask us to withdraw our missiles'.[46]

A flexible interpretation of the Montreux Convention

The question of the Straits constitutes the cornerstone of Turkish–Soviet relations. The regime governing passage through the Straits has historically been subject to different laws: exclusive sovereignty of Turkey (1453–1841), which used its discretionary right to allow or forbid passage; neutralization (1841–1914), which was designed to bar access to the Straits to all warships; internationalization (1918–36), which established the principle of freedom of passage for the naval forces of all countries.[47]

In 1936, disagreement surfaced between the two countries when the Montreux Convention on the Straits was under discussion. The USSR wanted complete freedom of passage for ships belonging to countries bordering the Black Sea and sought to limit the movements of ships belonging to other countries. Turkey on the other hand wanted to limit as much as possible – in war time – the number of foreign ships in the Straits, whether or not they belonged to countries bordering the Black Sea. In the end, the Montreux Convention authorized, in peace time, the passage of all ships with prior notification to the Ankara government: eight days for Black Sea powers and 15 days for the rest. In war time, if Turkey remained neutral, the warships of belligerents could not, except exceptionally as provided in the Convention, use the Straits. If Turkey was a belligerent or if it felt itself threatened, 'the passage of warships shall be left to the discretion of the [Ankara] government'.

Moscow was later to criticize Turkey for not having been able or willing to apply these provisions during the Second World War. In the note of 8 August 1946, mentioned above, the Kremlin asserted, citing a number of examples, that the Axis powers had been able to move their ships through the Straits. The Montreux Convention was thus outdated, as the three allied powers had recognized. For its part the USSR demanded that in war time, the Straits be always open to the passage of ships belonging to the Black Sea powers and forbidden to those of other powers. The regime of the Straits should be laid down by Turkey and the other Black Sea powers which 'shall organize joint means of defence'.

The Turkish government replied that it was ready to accept a revision of the Convention to take account of changes that had occurred in naval technology since 1936. Having always sought, in this matter as in others, to avoid dealing with the USSR alone, Turkish diplomacy wondered nevertheless whether 'the Soviet concept of a new regime for the Straits will continue to be based, with certain alterations designed apparently to attenuate its strictness, on the five points set out in the two notes of August and September 1946'.[48]

The thesis of B. Oran,[49] who protests against myths widespread in Turkey and the

West and argues that Tsarist Russia's interest in 'its south' was not to gain access to warm waters but to ensure its own security in the face of possible attacks by Western fleets, doubtless deserves particular attention for the period he considers. It must be recognized today, however, that the structure of conflict prevailing in the Mediterranean basin, the need to ensure a permanent presence in this sea ('showing the flag diplomacy') and the need to forestall possible military interventions by the American Sixth Fleet in the Middle East, make access to the Mediterranean an absolute necessity for the Soviets.

Since July 1976, Turkish governments have closed their eyes to the transit of ships of a type that contravene the clauses of the Montreux Convention (such as the 'Kiev' aircraft carriers, rechristened 'Yuri Gagarin' and 'Novorossiisk' anti-submarine cruisers). It seems that Ankara does not encounter much opposition from the Americans for these concessions to the Soviets. The Americans, moreover, hope, thanks to a very broad interpretation of the Montreux Convention, to have missile-equipped destroyers enter the Black Sea.[50]

The implicit quest for the USSR's support in disputes with Greece

Among the various approaches in international relations, the transnational paradigm stresses, as is well known, interdependence more than dependence, and the hierarchical, inegalitarian nature of the international system.[51] Conversely, the theory of dependence, like the theory of imperialism from which it derives, has a dialectical dimension which incorporates history.[52] The clientelist approach, closer to the second than to the transnational paradigm, has the merit, in our opinion, of stressing the dependence that characterizes the situation of some states with regard to others, while also drawing attention to the asymmetrical relations of vertical interaction that exist between them.

Thus, Greece, another client state of the Western world, has, especially since the fall of the colonels in 1974, been pursuing a policy towards the United States and the Soviet Union that is not basically different from Turkey's: negotiations to maintain the American military bases in return for increased economic and military aid from Washington; openings to the USSR in order to obtain, among other things, the necessary diplomatic support in dealing with Turkey.

The Cyprus affair was, as we suggested above, the reason for the reorientation of Turkish foreign policy. In 1963–64, the rulers in Ankara had at least four reasons to shift Turkey's foreign policy: they felt that no solution to the Cyprus problem satisfactory to Turkey would be found in the narrow framework of NATO; a rapprochement between Turkey and the USSR would deprive Archbishop Makarios of a powerful potential ally; at the United Nations, conversely, Turkey would gain support not only among the communist states but also in the ranks of the non-aligned countries; and finally it would obtain Soviet economic aid which would make up for the inadequacy of aid coming from the United States.

Even though these calculations turned out to be only partly accurate, Turkey, isolated in the Third World, nevertheless succeeded in softening the Soviets' attitude on the Cyprus conflict.[53] Moscow now recognized the existence in the island of 'two national communities', which practically amounted to rejecting *Enosis* (unification of the island with Greece). In return, Ankara supposedly assured Moscow that it would not oppose the demilitarization and neutralization of Cyprus, that is the removal of the British bases.

Subsequently, Turkey continued to seek out and stress Moscow's support. Certain Soviet initiatives, however, such as the proposal, formulated in August 1974, to call an international conference on the Cyprus problem, proved incompatible with the refusal of successive Turkish governments to internationalize the Cyprus problem. On the other apple of discord between Athens and Ankara, the delimitation of territorial waters in the Aegean Sea, the Soviet thesis is closer, juridically, to Greece's than to Turkey's.[54] The Soviets nevertheless seem to favour the latter, essentially for two reasons. In the first place, the Soviets feel that it is not in their interest openly to adopt an attitude favourable to Greece, Turkey being strategically more important. In the second place, if Athens' proposal to re-establish the 12-mile rule was to be adopted, the Aegean Sea would become a Greek lake, which might risk disturbing the movement of Soviet ships whose passage would depend on special authorization. In June 1978, fearing that Athens might grant Moscow 'free passage' (i.e. without the restrictions of 'innocent passage') through the corridors that the Soviet fleet uses today,[55] Bülent Ecevit offered the Soviets 'facilities'. He then tried to make it appear that faced with Greek 'revisionism', Turkish and Soviet interests coincided.

Obtaining economic aid without political strings

It is well known that, when they choose which countries they will trade with and which they will aid, Soviet leaders tend to prefer small countries or countries occupying an important strategic situation. Turkey is one of the latter; it is, in addition, the sole country in NATO to receive Soviet aid, and, in common with India, one of the largest beneficiaries of such aid among developing countries.

The principal object of the governments of Demirel's Justice Party after 1965 was economic development. This called for a certain degree of flexibility in foreign policy in order to optimize the possibilities of foreign investment. It was not a question of an anti-Western policy, but of pragmatic and realistic management,[56] along with the need to escape from the isolation born of the successive twists and turns of the Cyprus question. This policy was also dictated by the need to develop the Turkish economy and industry. It was in this perspective that economic agreements could be reached with the USSR.

Thanks to these cooperation agreements, Soviet assistance made it possible to carry out various large-scale projects, such as: the iron and steel complex at Iskenderun (the third largest Turkish steelworks and one of the largest projects financed by the Soviets outside the socialist bloc); the refinery at Aliaga near Izmir; the aluminium factory at Seydisehir; the wood fibre panel at Artvin; the sulphuric acid factory at Bandirma; and the joint construction of a water reservoir (still unfinished) on the Arpaçay river border. This Soviet assistance was accompanied by the granting of credits at very low rates of interest, amounting to several billion dollars, including 650 million in 1976.[57] In addition, Turkey received capital goods from the Soviet Union in exchange for its agricultural produce that was hard to export. But Moscow's refusal, in 1978, to grant oil on credit to the Ecevit government, at a time when Turkey was experiencing an acute need in this area, was interpreted in diplomatic circles and in the Turkish press, as a hesitation on the part of the USSR to give its blessing to a social-democratic experiment that it seemed to consider, 'from afar, like an ice block'.[58]

Whereas the pro-Soviet communist left felt that the economic rapprochement would have as a corollary a greater 'political rapprochement' which it also wanted to see, the ruling class, to avoid any political concessions, had no hesitation in restricting Soviet aid, in certain circumstances. This at any rate is what happened in 1980, the year of the Soviet intervention in Afghanistan and the military *coup d'état* in Turkey. Fearing the political implications of Soviet aid, Turkish rulers have always hesitated to accept Soviet military assistance, even though they have often stated that they would reject no offer of assistance 'wherever it comes from'. Thus, in April 1978, on the occasion of the visit by the Soviet chief of staff, Marshal Orgakov, Ankara declined a proposal for arms deliveries. Yet this proposal was in contradiction with Soviet policy of not, on principle, delivering weapons to 'bourgeois' or hostile contiguous countries.

* * *

'The importance of our strategic position, and the bravery of Mehmet[59] who lives on these lands, are still valid. That is why I am expecting from the honourable minister that it all be sold at a good price'.[60] It was in these crisp terms that, in the late 1940s, Y. K. Tengirsenk, former Minister of Foreign Affairs, speaking from the tribune of the National Assembly, called on his successor to think of Turkey's foreign policy. Turkish leaders, until the years that followed the military *coup d'état* of 1960, traumatized by Soviet demands, and linked to business circles, thought they could find security and economic aid in unconditional alignment with the West. This approach, based on complete disregard of the constraints of geography, dangerously exposed Turkey's national sovereignty at the time of the Cuban missile crisis and the U-2 affair. Turkey's wholly negative conception of the USSR in those days resulted from the close clientelist relationship between Turkey and the West.

This unfavourable perception was fuelled by a virulent anti-communism presented by the elites as being one of the essential components of Kemalism and by the age-old antagonism between the two countries. The persistence of this latter element is still, today, undeniable. The support won by the pan-Turkish and violently anti-Soviet National Action Party in the 1970s among ethnic Turkish populations in the eastern provinces which had experienced Russian occupation, is a sign of this.

These ideological factors nevertheless do not stand in the way of the 'good neighbour' policy begun with the USSR after 1963–64. The decline of the Soviet threat, the international climate of détente, the need to diversify external relations and the new questioning by the intelligentsia of the excessively dependent external policy pursued during the previous period, were the main causes of this. The economic self-centredness of the European Community, the powerlessness of

American presidents at odds with a Congress that was more pro-Greek than pro-Turkish (the embargo on arms destined for Turkey after the Cyprus crisis) simply accentuated this rapprochement. Anxious to use this as a means of pressure on the West without making it into the basis of an 'auction policy', Turkey equally rejected neutralism which would inevitably lead to 'Finlandization' because of the overwhelming Soviet military superiority. The Turks remain convinced that Moscow is, secretly, carrying out a policy of destabilization in their country – notably via Bulgaria through which enormous quantities of weapons were transported between 1975 and 1980 as, among other things, the recent twists in the inquiry into the attempted assassination of Pope John Paul II have revealed. All these reasons then led Turkish decision-makers to limit the extent of this rapprochement and go back to a certain Ottoman diplomatic tradition which consisted in avoiding dealing with Moscow alone and seeking Western protection.

Notes

1. On the subject of Ottoman–Russian relations, apart from the bibliography in Russian which is quite abundant, the most exhaustive, though very descriptive Turkish work is A. N. Kurat's, *Türkiye ve Rusya XVIII. Yüzyil sonundan Kurtulus savasina kadar Türk–Rus iliskileri*, Ankara, Türk Tarih Kurumu, 1970, which covers the period from 1798 to 1919. For Turkish–Soviet relations, there are a number of studies relating to the beginnings of the Kemalist period. See in particular, S. Yerasimos, *Türk Sovyet iliskileri (Ekim devriminden 'Milli Mücadele' ye)*, Istanbul, Gözlem yay., 1979; H. Z. Karal, 'Turkish relations with Soviet Russia during the National Liberation War of Turkey, 1918–1922: A study in the Diplomacy of the Kemalist Revolution', Ph.D. thesis, University of California, 1967; G. S. Harris, *The Origins of Communism in Turkey*, Stanford, Hoover Institution Publications, 1967; and the well documented article by P. Dumont, 'L'axe Moscou–Ankara. Les relations turco-soviétiques de 1919 à 1922', *Cahiers du Monde Russe et Soviétique*, XVIII, 3, July–September 1977, pp. 165–93. See also the memoirs of Mustafa Kemal's ambassador to Moscow, A. F. Cebesoy, *Moskova Hâtiralari*, Istanbul, Vatan Nesriyati, 1955.

For the more recent period see especially F. C. Erkin *Les relations turco-soviétiques et la question des Détroits*, Ankara, Basnur Matbaasi, 1968, which is also a testimony of the highest order from a figure who held the posts of Secretary General in the Ministry of Foreign Affairs and then Minister at crucial moments; B. Oran, 'Türkiye'nin 'Kuzey'deki Büyük Komsu' sorunu nedir?', *Siyasal Bilgiler Fakültesi Dergisi*, March 1970, vol. XXV, no. 1, pp. 41–93; K. Karpat, 'Turkish–Soviet relations', in K. Karpat et al., *Turkey's Foreign Policy in Transition, 1950–1974*, Leiden, E. J. Brill, 1975, pp. 73–107; M. P. Cabiaux, 'La Turquie et ses relations avec l'Union soviétique. Antécedents historiques et incidence sur l'engagement dans l'affrontement Est–Ouest', *Chroniques de politique étrangère*, vol. XIX, no 6, November 1966, pp. 615–730.

2. Quoted by M. Mitchell, *The Maritime History of Russia, 1848–1948*, London, Sidgwick and Jackson, 1949, p. 136.

3. Convinced that the Russians would not go so far as to launch an open conflict

with Turkey, Mustafa Kemal had let Moscow know the demands of the Grand Assembly on 1920 in raw terms: 'All the statistics relating to the provinces of Van and Bitlis, whether recent or old, show that there have always been proportionately fewer Armenians in these provinces than Muslims. In these circumstances, to demand the abandonment of a portion of the territory to a minority constitutes a typically imperialist action. Created to struggle against imperialism, the National Government in Ankara finds itself obliged to reject this demand.' A. F. Cebesoy, *Moskova Hâtiralari*, op. cit., p. 90. French tr. in P. Dumont, 'L'axe Moscou–Ankara', op. cit., p. 175. The Armenian question implicitly occupied a not unimportant place in Turkish–Soviet relations. On this subject see R. H. Dekmijian 'Soviet Turkish relations and politics in the Armenian SSR', *Soviet Studies*, 19, April 1968, pp. 510–25, which sets out the attitude of intellectuals in Soviet Armenia to the rapprochement between Turkey and the USSR.

4. *La Turquie devant la guerre (Mission à Ankara, 1939–1940)*, Paris, Plon, 1964, p. 335.

5. A. F. Cebesoy, *Milli mücadele hâtiralari*, Istanbul, Vatan Nesriyati, 1953, p. 475. Quoted in P. Dumont, 'L'axe Moscou–Ankara', op. cit., p. 174 (our emphasis).

6. See G. Jaschke, 'Le rôle du communisme dans les relations russo–turques de 1919 à 1922', *Orient*, 26, 1963, pp. 31–44.

7. For all these organizations as well as for the 'official' Turkish Communist Party, see P. Dumont, 'La révolution impossible. Les courants d'opposition en Anatolie. 1920–1921', *Cahiers du Monde russe et soviétique*, XIX, 1–2, January–February 1978, pp. 143–74.

8. Ibid., p. 163.

9. On Mustapha Suphi's Communist Party, see P. Dumont, 'Bolchevisme et Orient. Le Parti communiste turc de Mustapha Suphi 1918–1921', *Cahiers du Monde Russe et Soviétique*, XVIII, 4, October–December 1977, pp. 377–409 and T. Z. Tunaya, *Türkiye'de de siyasî partiler, 1859–1952*, Istanbul, Dogan Kardes yay., 1952, pp. 358–68.

For a more recent assessment, see: G. Hermet and J.-F. Bayart, 'Die Kommunistische Partei der Turkeï', in H. Timmermann et al., *Die Kommunistischen Parteien Südeuropas*, Baden-Baden, Nomos Verlagsgesellschaft, 1979, pp. 383–405.

10. See Chris Kutschera, 'La poudrière kurde. Faiblesses d'une résistance divisée, *Le Monde Diplomatique*, September 1980.

11. Pan-Turanianism advocates the unity of the Turkish–Mongol and Finno-Hungarian peoples in an anti-Slav synthesis, whereas pan-Turkism is limited to uniting the Turkish peoples. On this question, the literature is relatively abundant. See in particular, A. Bennigsen and C. L. Quelquejay, *Les mouvements nationaux chez les musulmans de Russie*, Paris–The Hague, Mouton, 1960; C. W. Hostler, *Turkism and the Soviets*, London, G. Allen and Unwin, 1957; H. Carrère d'Encausse and S. Schram, *Le marxisme et l'Asie, 1853–1964*, Paris, A. Colin, 1965 (Eng. tr., *Marxism and Asia*, London, Allen Lane, The Penguin Press, 1969); S. A. Zenkovsky, *Pan-Turkism and Islam in Russia*, Cambridge, Mass., Harvard University Press, 1967; and the recent work by J. M. Landau, *Pan-Turkism in Turkey, A study of irredentism*, London, C. Hurst, 1981.

12. P. Dumont, 'La fascination du bolchevisme. Enver pacha et le parti des soviets populaires, 1919–1922', *Cahiers de Monde Russe et Soviétique*, XVI, 2, April–June 1975, p. 151.

13. To this can be added the Turkomans, Kirghizes, Bashkirs, Karakalpaks,

Koumyks, Uighurs, Karatchaïs, Balkars and Nogaïs. On this subject see the recent work by A. Benningsen and C. L. Quelquejay, *Les Musulmans oubliés*, Paris, Maspero, 1981, pp. 75 et seq.

14. J.-F. Médard, 'Le rapport de clientèle, du phénomène social à l'analyse politique', *Revue française de science politique*, February 1976, pp. 128–31.

15. In 1947, at a session of the UN General Assembly, when the Soviet delegate had treated the Turkish vote as an American manipulation, Selim Sarper, the head of the Turkish delegation, declared 'Finally, we are going to vote for the American proposal, while being happy and even proud to be in the same camp as the United States' (*Ayin tarihi*, November 1947, no 168, p. 19). Quoted by M. Gök, 'L'attitude de la Turquie en face de la décolonisation: 1945–1965', Doctorat d'État in political science, Paris, University of Paris I, 1978, p. 7.

16. Claire Sterling's 'analysis' reflects this clientelist relationship very well in all its dimensions, including the affective one: 'Contrary to the rule that no one is grateful to his benefactor, they (the Turks) loved and admired us, they welcomed our troops, listened to our advice, endorsed every one of our actions in Korea, Cuba, Vietnam; and not once, in 18 years, have they broken the windows of an American library', 'Ankara: Inönü looks left', *The Reporter*, 9 September 1965, p. 18. Quoted by Cabiaux, op. cit., p. 665. When in 1964, Turkey manifested some inclination to disengage from its American protector, the United States lost, according to the same author, 'that extra quality of unconditional loyalty from one of the few nations still disposed to offer it', ibid., p. 18. quoted in Cabiaux, op. cit., p. 695.

17. F. C. Erkin, *Les relations turco-soviétiques*, op. cit., p. 234.

18. Ibid., pp. 169 et seq.

19. A. R. Deluca, *Great Power Rivalry at the Turkish Straits: the Montreux Conference and Convention of 1936*, Boulder, 1981, p. 149.

20. See among others, J.-B. Duroselle, *Histoire diplomatique de 1919 à nos jours*, Paris, Dalloz, 1974, p. 459; F. C. Erkin *Les relations turco-soviétiques*, op. cit., p. 295; E. Weisband, *Turkish Foreign Policy, 1943–1945: Small state diplomacy and great power politics*, Princeton, Princeton University Press, 1973, pp. 315 et seq. The historical accuracy of these demands is violently disputed by certain pro-Soviet circles in Turkey. On this, see the lengthy but insufficiently documented and not very convincing 'theses on Turkey', by an academic, Y. Kücük, *Türkiye üzerine tezler (1908–1978)*, Istanbul, Tekin yay., 1979, vol. II, passim, which sees in these demands a 'myth', or even machinations by the Turkish leaders of the time to justify Turkey's integration into the West. The territorial demands were, according to the author, the work of a number of 'irresponsible' Georgian professors. See also in the same vein, the article by the former ambassador and ex-president of the 'Committee for Peace', M. Dikerdem, 'Soguk savas ve Türkiye', *Sosyalist iktidar*, no 5, February 1980, pp. 28–34 and C. Alsan, *Türk–Sovyet Halklarinin Kardesliği*, Istanbul, Sorun yay., 1976. Alsan scarcely mentions the Soviet demands on the Straits and the eastern provinces, except to say that the idea of 'a threat from the north' was created from scratch in order to bind Turkey solidly to the West. It is to be noted also that the author endeavours to preserve Mustafa Kemal's personality in the eyes of the communists, and blames the physical elimination of the Turkish communists on 'the right-wing of the party which had taken over all political power in the country' (pp. 31 et seq.).

21. F. C. Erkin, *Les relations turco-soviétiques*, op. cit., p. 324.

22. On this subject see the testimony – despite its being rather vague – of a

journalist well-connected in ruling circles on what he calls the '1945 nightmare', M. Toker, *Türkiye üzerinde 1945 kâbusu*, Ankara, Akis yay., 1971, pp. 61 and 88 et seq.

23. J.-P. Derriennic, *Le Moyen-orient au XXe siècle*, Paris, A. Colin, 1980, p. 131.

24. See the article by a clear-sighted observer, A. S. Esmer, 'Türkiye' yi Amerika'mi kurtardi?', *Yön*, 25 March 1966.

25. Quoted by Cabiaux, op. cit., pp. 672–3 which quotes T. Çadircioğlu, *La Turquie et l'intégration progressive de l'Europe*, Lausanne, Imprimerie vaudoise, 1961, p. 125.

26. S. Bilge et al., *Olaylarla Türk dis politikasi (1919–1965)*, Ankara, SBF yay., 1969, p. 334.

27. For the full text of the note see Cabiaux, op. cit., p. 680.

28. *Olaylarla*, op. cit., pp. 294–95.

29. J.-P. Derriennic, *Le Moyen-Orient au XXe siècle*, op. cit., p. 143.

30. J.-F. Bayart, 'La politique extérieure de la Turquie: les espérances déçues', *Revue française de science politique*, October–December 1981, pp. 861–89.

31. Ibid., p. 871.

32. Ibid.

33. *Géopolitique et géostratégie*, Paris, PUF, 1969, p. 31.

34. See J.-P. Derriennic, *Le Moyen-Orient au XXe siècle*, op. cit., p. 142.

35. An intensive change of delegations resulted in the visits: to Moscow by the Turkish Minister of Foreign Affairs, in January 1965; to Ankara by Mr Podgorny; and in August 1965, the Turkish Prime Minister, Mr Urgüplü, to Moscow. Since that date, these visits have continued to take place regularly.

36. D. Sezer, *Kamuoyu ve Dis Politika*, Ankara, SBF yay., 1972, pp. 305 et seq.

37. D. Sezer, *Turkey's Security Policies*, London, IISS, Adelphi Papers, 1981, p. 2.

38. *Temps nouveaux*, 23, 1978, p. 13.

39. See the Turkish press of the time and *Le Monde* of 22 June 1978.

40. I. Cem, *Tarih açisindan 12 mart*, Istanbul, Cem yay., 1977, vol. II, pp. 35–6. The daily *Hürriyet* of 5 January 1971 had even suggested that the CIA was concerned by rumours that Turkey had granted Soviet Migs flying to Egypt refuelling rights at Turkish aerodromes. Denied by the authorities, such rumours might have been the work of the American secret services, as Cem stresses, op. cit., p. 35.

41. 'Turkey is a bit more co-operative' noted *The Economist* of 11 December 1982 before adding about the bases 'The official line is that they [three new bases] are for NATO operations but the Americans are clearly counting on the Turks' support in any crisis in Southwest Asia'.

42. Note addressed by the Soviet government to the Turkish government, 13 May 1960, following the U-2 incident. *La Documentation Française, Articles et documents*, no. 0.964, daily texts, pp. 1–2, Paris, 25 June 1960.

43. See *Le Monde*, 16 May 1979, 26 June 1979 and 13 July 1979.

44. B. J. Bernstein, 'The Cuban missile crisis: trading the Jupiters in Turkey?', *Political Science Quarterly*, vol. 95, no 1, Spring 1980, p. 101.

45. *Cahiers de l'Orient contemporain*, December 1962, quoted by Cabiaux, op. cit., p. 685.

46. Bernstein, op. cit., pp. 119–20.

47. For more details, see F. C. Erkin, *Les relations turco-soviétiques*, op. cit., pp. 21–69.

48. Ibid., p. 421.

49. Oran, op. cit., p. 46.

50. E. Young and V. Sebek, 'Red Sea and Blue Oceans: Soviet uses of Ocean Law', *Survival*, 1978/6, p. 258.

51. See J. H. Leurdijk, 'From international to transnational politics: a change of paradigms?', *International Social Science Journal*, vol. XXVI, no. 1, 1974, pp. 58–75.

52. See M. Kaplan, 'The structure of power in international relations', *International Social Science Journal*, vol. XXVI, no. 1, 1974, pp. 104–17.

53. On this, see A. Aziz, 'Sovyetlerin Kibris tutumlari, 1965–1970', *Siyasal Bilgiler Fakültesi Dergisi* vol. XXIV, December 1969, pp. 201–44.

54. I. Valinakis, 'La politique soviétique a l'égard de la Turquie: 1964–1978', Mémoire de science politique, Paris, University of Paris, I, 1979, p. 68.

55. Ibid.

56. I. Cem, *Tarih açisindan 12 mart*, op. cit., p. 18.

57. *Le Monde*, 22 June 1978.

58. M.A. Birand, in *Milliyet*, 23 October 1979.

59. The usual nickname of the Turkish soldier.

60. Quoted by Oran, op. cit., p. 168.

4 The USSR as seen by the ASEAN Countries

Françoise Cayrac-Blanchard

If one asks how the Soviet Union is seen by the Association of South East Asian Nations (ASEAN), and what sort of relations the latter hopes to maintain with it, the analysis can be conducted at three levels. First, define what ASEAN is and what the specific factors are that guide its attitudes towards the great powers and the communist countries. Then, examine the type of relations that exist between the USSR and ASEAN. Last and not least, distinguish the perceptions that have developed about the Indo-China problem which constitutes a high priority question for ASEAN. This problem, closely bound up with its security and the future of the region, has, as a consequence of the Soviet-Vietnamese alliance and the occupation of Cambodia by Vietnam, given a more concrete and immediate character to a 'Soviet threat' which is, however, still perceived very differently by the five partners in ASEAN.

ASEAN or the non-communist nations of South-East Asia in quest of a difficult neutrality

The creation of ASEAN in Bangkok, on 8 August 1967, was made possible by the change of political direction in Indonesia in 1966, following the army's seizure of power. Indonesia is indisputably the regional great power in terms of its size, population and resources.[1] Until then, the creation of an organization of this type had been blocked by the anti-imperialist policy of Sukarno who relied on the Indonesian Communist Party (so much so, said some, that he paved its road to power), wanted to adapt Marxism to Indonesian conditions, had created the Djakarta–Beijing axis and launched total confrontation against 'neocolonial Greater Malaysia'. General Suharto's swing to a pro-Western position and the reconciliation with Malaysia, on the contrary, made possible the formation of ASEAN which, in addition to Malaysia and Indonesia, includes Thailand, the Philippines, Singapore and, since 1984, Brunei. Occurring just when a negotiated solution to the Vietnam conflict was beginning to appear possible, the creation of ASEAN, which from the very beginning enjoyed the sympathy of the United States, fitted well into an American strategy of containment of China. The Five were in fact states that were economically – and, in varying degrees, militarily – linked to the United States, which for its part wanted to see regimes, capable of assuring the necessary stability and order to prevent the development of communism, keep themselves in power there, even if this involved a few deviations from democracy.

ASEAN, at first limited to economic and cultural cooperation (and even this was not very active), took on a new political dimension after 1971 under the impetus of Malaysia; this followed the appearance of two new international factors directly affecting the region. First, Great Britain's withdrawal from east of Suez, announced by London in 1967–68, meant that there would no longer be any British troops in South-East Asia after 1971 and that the British bases in the Malayan peninsula and Singapore would be closed. That was a decision that was bound to worry Malaysia, which had barely recovered from its 'confrontation' with Indonesia. Almost simultaneously, American policy too was shifting towards disengagement, with the decision to 'Vietnamize' the war in Indo-China, and Nixon's announcement of the Guam doctrine in July 1969. In turn, the Sino-American rapprochement of 1972 contributed to a major shift in the balance of power in Asia, just when the outlines of the post-Vietnam situation were beginning to emerge.

What would ASEAN do faced with these moves by the great powers? Did the vacuum left by the United States, which was playing on reconciliation with China, risk being filled by the Soviet Union which, hoping in its turn to contain China, was proposing a collective security system in Asia and extending its influence in South-East Asia (Soviet–Indian treaty of August 1971)? Or by China? Should an attempt be made to secure a reduction of the great power presence in the region or, on the contrary, to work towards a balance of that presence? Did the ASEAN countries risk finding themselves alone to provide for their defence?

Even if things had not yet reached that point, Malaysia, while, along with Singapore, seeking assurances from Australia and New Zealand, deemed it urgent to take a position diplomatically. Meeting in Kuala Lumpur in November 1971, to lay the foundations of a common position, the five ASEAN members expressed their determination to obtain from the great powers (United States, China, USSR) recognition of South-East Asia as a 'Zone of Peace, Freedom and Neutrality, free from any form or manner of interference by outside Powers'.[2] From this point, they were inviting the countries of the region to associate themselves with this aim if they so wished. But Vietnam was not ready to hear this appeal.

The communist victories of 1975 in Indo-China, and the end of the Second Vietnam War, suddenly gave this proposal for the neutralization of South-East Asia, whose achievement had not moved the least bit closer, a new actuality. South-East Asia appeared more than ever divided into two antagonistic blocs: communist Indo-China and anti-communist ASEAN, denounced by Hanoi as a second SEATO (South-East Asia Treaty Organization).

This accusation derived from a rather facile simplification. Of course, ASEAN remains an anti-communist organization. But it has chosen not to move towards a military defence pact similar to SEATO, even if this solution remains a standing temptation for some.[3] It seeks rather a neutralization of the region, which involves pursuing a policy of balanced relations with the great powers present in the region.

While the ASEAN countries perceive the threat as coming principally from the communist countries (USSR, China, Vietnam), they do not all analyse it in the same way. None of them expects an all-out attack conducted by the USSR, China or

Vietnam – even if in 1975 some Indonesian generals raised the possible risk of an attack by their Vietnamese neighbour, now become a military power. The danger is seen rather as coming from subversion based on rebel movements capable of destabilizing the existing regimes.

The fact is that these countries are experiencing serious problems which could threaten their stability or national cohesion. They are, at least as regards three of them, authoritarian regimes. In Indonesia, a military regime has been vainly trying to give itself the trappings of democracy. The army dominates the political and economic life of the country and the opposition, divided between Muslims and nationalists, has fewer and fewer legal rights. In the Philippines, President Marcos ruled as strong man till 1986, relying for support on the army, business circles and . . . his own family. The constant progress of a guerilla war, waged partly by an autonomist Muslim movement in Mindanao, but above all by a communist movement resurgent since 1968, combined with worsening economic and social problems, and the scandal surrounding the assassination of his political rival, Ninoy Aquino, steadily weakened Marcos. In February 1986, Cory Aquino, the Presidential candidate of the liberal opposition, supported by the powerful Catholic Church, managed to impose electoral defeat upon him. Abandoned by the Army and by the Americans, Marcos was forced to flee. Politically fragile, but successfully resisting a putchist army, the new President is striving, admittedly with little effect so far, to achieve national reconciliation and to promote economic revival, with American support. In Singapore, a strong parliamentary regime has, since 1959, been dominated by Lee Kuan Yew. His People's Action Party which has come to hold a quasi-monopoly of seats in parliament leaves scarcely any scope for institutional opposition or social challenges. In Thailand, where violent crisis follows violent crisis, the military dictatorship gave way to a civilian democracy in 1973, but since 1976, it has had a semi-parliamentary, semi-authoritarian system, a sort of democracy under military supervision. The existence of a number of factions within the army itself, and a tradition of *coups d'état*, contribute to making the regime rather fragile. In Malaysia, parliamentary democracy is more firmly established. Governments have succeeded one another without problems. It is the ethnic problem (35% Chinese, who, economically, dominate 54% Malays, in the peninsula) that is the country's weak point.

What about communist movements among the Five? Could they constitute a source of influence for the Soviet Union? In Indonesia, the coming to power of the military rested on the liquidation of the communists. The PKI (Indonesian Communist Party), which had espoused the Maoist line after 1963, was banned. Its supporters were massacred or kept in camps for 14 years. Today, the survivors, now free but closely watched, show little sign of wanting to resume political activity. Yet communist groups continue to exist in exile, in Beijing and Moscow. Each is closely watched by the host country, and it is difficult to assess how representative they are. In Thailand, the Communist Party of Thailand, reinforced by the influx of many students after 1976, found itself weakened and divided by the Sino-Vietnamese conflict. Called on by Beijing to cooperate with the Bangkok government against Hanoi's 'hegemonism', it suffered serious internal dissensions and numerous defections. A recent tendency ('Pak Mai' or New Party) has moved towards a rapprochement with Hanoi; it has not assumed much importance. For its part, Bangkok deems that it has put an end to the armed struggle.[4] As for the Communist Party of Malaysia, which has sought refuge in southern Thailand, it too is pro-Chinese. It was very active, in the mid-1970s, carrying out urban terrorism. Kuala Lumpur estimates its strength at about 2,000, but fears that it might exploit peasant discontent or infiltrate Islamic fundamentalism[5] which constitutes the most active opposition to the Kuala Lumpur regime. In the Philippines, a new leadership of the CP, after 1968, has adopted a Maoist-inspired line oriented towards armed struggle. The Party has set up a military organization, the New People's Army (NPA) which is particularly active in the centre of Luzon, in Samar, Panay and Negros, where it enjoys popular support. The movement has partially allied itself with the Moro National Liberation Front (MNLF) which operates in Mindanao and calls for the creation of a separatist Muslim state. Marcos accepted to negotiate with the MNLF, while engaging in a brutal but ineffective repression against the NPA. In 1986 the Filipino communists did not back Cory Aquino, but later changed their view and accepted to negotiate with her, although with no result as yet. In Singapore since the late 1960s, Lee Kuan Yew has been able to silence all left-wing opposition. It is thus unlikely that these opposition movements can or want to serve as channels for Soviet influence.

To the Five, the Soviet Union is the carrier of a dangerous and condemned ideology. In Indonesia not only the Communist Party but the teaching of Marxism–Leninism has been banned since 1966. The military urgently feels the need to develop an ideological line that would block the possibility of a reappearance of Marxist doctrine which would directly challenge the regime's options in all areas. Communism remains synonymous with atheism; the communists imprisoned after 1965 underwent an intensive religious indoctrination, aimed at correcting thought processes.[6]

The stability of the Five remains tied up with their economic success. Singapore, which modelled itself on Japan, is the most favoured: its trading and industrial activities give it the highest per capita income in Asia after Japan. But the other four find their development compromised by the oil crisis (in the case of Indonesia) and the fall in raw material prices. Despite quite satisfactory growth rates until the recent world recession, ever deeper social inequalities have provoked growing discontent, which is especially perceptible in Indonesia. This feeling of social injustice, aggravated by the corruption among the ruling leadership, is a factor working against political stability in the long term.

In Indonesia and Malaysia especially, the existence of Islamic opposition movements tinged with fundamentalism, helps make the attitude of these states towards the communist countries even more prudent: in addition to the concern not to provide arguments for these Muslim extremists, the danger of a tactical alliance (or infiltration) between Islam and communism, as in the Philippines, is felt as an ever-present possibility.

The fact that Malaysia and Indonesia have influential Chinese minorities (only 3% of the population in Indonesia, but, as in Malaysia, playing a dominant economic role) creates a particular type of relation with China which is seen as the potential source of their manipulation. It is a factor which weighs heavily in the assessment of the dangers and which explains why, in Djakarta and Kuala Lumpur, fear of China seems to be stronger than fear of the Soviet Union.[7] The situation is reversed in the case of Singapore where 75% of the population is Chinese.

But, above all, it is the pro-Western commitment of the five members of ASEAN that negatively conditions their relations with the communist countries. Their model of development, aid received, investment, commercial exchanges, all bind them to the West and more particularly to the United States and Japan, even if some of them are trying to diversify their exchanges towards the EEC; it is the same with military aid. But in this latter area, some ASEAN members have committed themselves further than others. The Philippines, historically the state most strongly linked to the United States, still has two major American bases on its territory; like Thailand, it sent troops to Vietnam. Conversely, in Thailand, a process of withdrawal of American forces, begun in 1969, became effective in July 1976. Yet in 1975 these two states agreed to the dissolution of SEATO, although they remain linked to the United States through the Manila treaty. Indonesia has succeeded in remaining apparently more neutral, refusing both to send troops to Vietnam or to open American bases on its soil. As for Malaysia, it opted, after the British withdrawal, for neutralization. Finally, Singapore has been content to give Washington verbal support.

Geographical situation also plays a part in the perception of a possible Soviet or Chinese threat. Thailand, a front-line state since 1979 by virtue of its border with Cambodia, which no longer acts as a buffer-state, cannot have the same view of the danger as have the archipelagos, such as Indonesia and the Philippines, that are further removed from the conflict. Similarly, the fact that the Soviet Union is far away and China relatively close, and that China historically considers South-East Asia as its sphere of influence, conditions the perception that the Five have of these two countries.

It should be stressed, too, that one of the strong cards ASEAN holds is its unity. Each of its members is well aware of this and thus appears determined to defend it. While the Indo-China crisis sometimes exacerbated the internal divergences of the association, overall it strengthened this cohesion.

Relations between ASEAN and the USSR

South-East Asia is far from being a priority for the Soviet Union, and the member countries of ASEAN are fully aware of that. At the beginning of the 1960s, the support given by Moscow to Sukarno's Indonesia, marked notably by the supply of a large quantity of military aid, reflected a willingness to be present in the region. The USSR supported the Indonesian claim to West Irian, which had remained in Dutch hands, and, with much less enthusiasm, Sukarno's confrontation with Malaysia. This policy failed because Indonesia chose a rapprochement with Mao's China[8] and, subsequently, the seizure of power by the military marked the end of communist influence in the country for a long time. Apart from this Indonesian sally, the USSR was for a long time not present in the region.

Starting in the 1970s, however, there was a reawakening of Soviet interest in Asia and the beginning of a global strategy in the region: in 1969 Leonid Brezhnev proposed a collective security system in Asia. Although formulated in very vague terms, this plan offered the countries of Asia non-military cooperation based on the principles of peaceful coexistence. In addition, it was designed to assure the stability of the region by protecting it from outside influences.[9]

In the West, this proposal has generally been seen as part of the determination of the USSR to assert and legitimize its presence and responsibilities in Asia, to contain China and by the same token to reduce the influence of the United States. In South-East Asia, the sole manifestation of this plan would, for the present, seem to be the Soviet–Vietnamese treaty of November 1978, although, unlike the Soviet–Afghan treaty of December 1978, it makes no explicit mention of it.

The ASEAN countries did not react to the Soviet proposal, except, in 1971, themselves to propose the creation of a 'Zone of Peace, Freedom and Neutrality' in South-East Asia. In fact what they wanted was to keep the USSR at arm's length and in no event put themselves into a position of dependence vis-à-vis the USSR. Instrumentally, the USSR continues above all to be seen as the great power in 'the other camp'. Its intentions are suspect, and its proposals are seen as designed to extend its influence. Yet a direct attack is not feared, and an Indonesian personality could say ingenuously of the increased Soviet naval presence in the Indian Ocean: 'Oh! Those few ships . . .' At the same time, Indonesia, Malaysia, Thailand and the Philippines refused to allow the Soviet navy to use their ports (September 1979), which on the other hand are open to the Seventh fleet.

The major risk remains subversion. But, without being totally non-existent, this risk probably comes less from the USSR than from China, given the dominant orientation of the communist parties in these countries. This is a positive point in favour of the USSR, especially when Beijing asserts, as Zhao Ziyang did in August 1981, that it continues to give these parties its 'moral and political support', much to the displeasure of the ASEAN countries. But when, as at the beginning of 1982, Radio Moscow broadcast statements emanating from the PKI in exile, Djakarta could not fail to be irritated, and demonstrations took place in front of the Soviet embassy in the Indonesian capital. At about the same time, a series of spy cases, involving the Soviets, broke in Malaysia, Indonesia and Singapore. The Indonesians, who declared that they were in full control of the situation, did not seem to be overly worried by such activities. These sorts of cases were rather messages in the form of warnings addressed to the Soviet partner. They have not, in any event, resulted in diplomatic crises, except perhaps in Malaysia where the Political Secretary to the Prime Minister was involved.[10]

Another factor, which also tends to limit relations between the ASEAN countries and the USSR, lies in the very low level of commercial exchanges.[11] The USSR is a third-ranking economic partner, and cannot be looked upon by ASEAN as a possible alternative for adjusting the American and Japanese preponderance in this area, as the EEC is for example. Furthermore, there is little liking for the barter form of these exchanges. Soviet aid is practically non-existent, and possible development projects – as in the case of Malaysia and Indonesia – are viewed with reservations by the recipients who fear encouraging a Soviet presence that would be more difficult to control.[12]

On the other hand, and rather curiously, it is in the most anti-Soviet of the Five, Singapore, that the Soviet Union is best established. Since 1968, it has had a trading company, South Union, and since 1971, a shipping company – Sinsov – with joint participation, which underwent rapid growth associated with the development of Soviet shipping services to Asia: in 1977 almost 100 Soviet ships called in at Singapore. In 1975, a Soviet–Singaporean fishing company was formed. Since 1971 there has also been a branch of the Moscow Narodny Bank in Singapore. Joint shipping companies also exist in Thailand and the Philippines, but they appear to be much less active.

If, basically, the ASEAN countries harbour reservations and mistrust towards the USSR, they also showed a spirit of openness after 1971 when they were trying to rebalance their external relations. But three of the Five have established official relations with the Soviet Union only recently.

As for Thailand, whose relations with the USSR are long established, it showed its willingness to be open even though its policy later leaned towards favouring China. With the end of the military dictatorship (1973) and the emergence in 1975 of a Vietnam – the traditional enemy – liberated from war and reunited, Bangkok reduced its relations with the United States, established diplomatic relations with China in July 1975, and simultaneously developed good relations with the USSR. Kukrit Pramoj, Prime Minister from March 1975 to April 1976, the main architect of this policy, noted that 'as a superpower the Soviet Union obviously has interests in this region and that the great potential is there for the Soviets to play a significant role that would be consonant with the interests of the regional powers'.[13] The rapprochement remained limited, however, Bangkok clearly not being about to commit itself to the 'collective security system in Asia'. Succeeding the violently anti-communist Thanin government (October 1976–October 1977), General Kriangsak resumed a more open 'independent foreign policy'. Thus, in March 1979, after having been to Washington, he was the first Thai head of government of Thailand to travel to Moscow, to obtain assurances on Vietnam's policy. Later, because of the evolution of the Cambodian problem, Bangkok chose to move closer to Beijing, which gave it a number of guarantees. The Thai military, already unpleasantly surprised by the appearance of the Soviet aircraft carrier *Minsk* in the Gulf of Siam in 1980, are very much disturbed by the fact that Moscow's naval presence in the South China Sea might take on a permanent character from the base at Cam Ranh.[14]

The Philippines, too, has manifested a desire to open up its relations. It opened diplomatic relations with China in June 1975 and then with the USSR in June 1976, the chronological order perhaps reflecting the order of priorities. On the other hand, Malaysia, which had established diplomatic relations with China in May 1974, had opened them with the USSR as early as 1968. In 1977, the Prime Minister, Hussein Onn, felt that Moscow could 'contribute to promoting peace and stability' in South-East Asia. A few years later, his successor, Datuk Sri Mahathir Mohamad, explained the limits of the opening towards the communist powers when he said: '. . . nor do we differentiate really between the role of China and the role of the Soviet Union. Both are equally disruptive. We want to keep them at arm's length', while his Minister of Foreign Affairs specified: 'The USSR is a global threat, China a regional threat.'[15] This conviction dominates the Malaysian policy of keeping a balance between the communist great powers. It rests on the need to avoid becoming involved in the Sino-Soviet conflict even if for Kuala Lumpur the principal danger remains Chinese.

Indonesia makes a similar analysis. It feels however that the Soviet and Chinese presence in South-East Asia is inevitable, while hoping that this presence does not remain limited to the military domain alone.[16] The Suharto regime, which has frozen its relations with China since 1967, had also put a brake on its relations with the USSR after 1965. It subsequently had to negotiate with Moscow a difficult rescheduling of Indonesian debt repayments; relations since then have been correct but cold. Soviet development aid projects proposed in about 1975 have remained obstinately shelved. Otherwise, Indonesia does not seem to be particularly perturbed by an increased Soviet presence in the waters of the region, on condition that the US presence is maintained. The fact of identifying China as the principal danger is something on which Indonesia agrees with the USSR. This is reinforced by the concern of both countries about the development of Japan's military power.[17] For Djakarta, which is endeavouring not to appear to be too overtly kowtowing to the United States, relations with Moscow are a means of giving some content to its non-alignment. This is notably seen in the carefully balanced programme of official visits and declarations such as that to *Asiaweek* by the Indonesian Minister of Foreign Affairs (4 May 1986): 'We are non-aligned and we feel that if the Americans have base facilities in the Philippines, there could be no objections to the Russians having them in Vietnam. It's no threat to us.' On the other hand, Djakarta does not at all like Moscow's support at the UN for resolutions condemning its occupation of East Timor (a former Portuguese colony annexed by Indonesia in 1976) nor the fact that its warships and submarines move through the Indonesian straits without always informing Indonesia in advance.[18]

Unlike Indonesia, Singapore identifies the Soviet danger as the dominant one and denounces it forcefully on every possible occasion. For S. Rajaratnam, former Minister of Foreign Affairs, then Deputy Prime Minister, the USSR is only aiming at extending its power. If it were to succeed in dominating Western Asia and laying its hands on world oil resources, it could destroy the three bastions of capitalism, Europe, Japan and the United States, without war. In South-East Asia its aim is seen as being the control of the vital Strait of Malacca.[19] This denunciation of the growing influence of the USSR, which Singapore has also taken up in the non-aligned movement, enables it to call for the continuation of a Western presence in South-East Asia. In 1976, Rajaratnam felt, moreover, that 'the only rational course for Southeast Asian nations is not to work for the liquidation of great power presence in the region but rather to ensure a multipower presence as a more agreeable alternative to a single power dominance'.[20]

This rapid survey of the positions of the ASEAN countries makes it possible to grasp the varying perceptions of the Soviet danger, and also to bring out their common denominator: a feeling of mistrust and a concern to limit Soviet influence in the region as much as possible. This latter concern seems all the greater today now that the Cambodian conflict has strengthened the Soviet presence in South-East Asia.

The Indo-China conflict

The end of the Vietnam war had inspired ASEAN to assert itself as a political force (with the summits at Bali and Kuala Lumpur in 1976 and 1977), while marking its concern to strengthen its special links with the Western powers and Japan.

The beginning of the China–Vietnam conflict drove the two rival communist blocs to court ASEAN: Vietnam, which had initially manifested hostility to the idea of ZOPFAN, now asserted its peaceful intentions and committed itself not to aid subversive movements in these countries. The USSR for its part wanted to encourage ASEAN's potential for resistance to Chinese influence. Finally, China pushed ASEAN to resist any hegemonisms.

The sudden alliance between the USSR and an increasingly isolated Vietnam (November 1978), the Vietnamese intervention in Cambodia and the military occupation of that country suddenly brought the danger of an armed confrontation to the Thai border.

ASEAN then spelled out its position. It condemned the 'armed intervention', demanded 'the immediate and complete withdrawal of foreign troops from Cambodia' (this has been modified since) and regarded the Khmers Rouges as the legitimate government in Cambodia. But while from 1979 to the present day, ASEAN has maintained a united policy, the divergences of view among its members have not disappeared and have in some cases even deepened. Should Vietnam be considered as the USSR's 'errand boy'?[21] Does the Vietnamese advance in the Indo-Chinese peninsula reflect a global Soviet strategy or a regional Vietnamese policy? The perception of the USSR by the countries of ASEAN has become inextricably bound up with their attitude towards the other great powers (China and the United States), their assessment of Vietnam and their vision of the future of South-East Asia. Which is the principal threat: Vietnam, the USSR's ally, or China?

Thailand, where General Prem succeeded General Kriangsak in March 1980, feels the Vietnamese threat most keenly, both in the risk of armed conflict spreading to its territory and in the problem of refugees flooding towards its border. For Thailand, the Vietnamese danger is closely tied up with the Soviet danger: Russian warships enjoy facilities in the Vietnamese bases at Cam Ranh and Da Nang and the Cambodian port of Kompong Som, and a Soviet aircraft carrier entered the Gulf of Siam for the first time in November 1980. Following the Soviet intervention in Afghanistan, Thailand immediately proposed reactivating a regional military alliance. But this idea ran into opposition from some of its partners, in particular Indonesia.[22]

While requesting (and obtaining) arms from the United States, Thailand feels itself deprived of American protection and it judges that China provides it with worthwhile guarantees against Vietnam. Chinese support has been precious in Bangkok's struggle against the CPT (Communist Party of Thailand). But by playing this game, Thailand has been dragged into aiding the Khmers Rouges, which considerably enhances the risks of the conflict spreading towards its territory and aids the growth of the influence of the great powers in the region.

Singapore is at one with Thailand, in that it is convinced that the USSR, having a capacity for intervention that China lacks, is the principal danger. Its leaders, too, have stressed the links between the cases of Afghanistan and Cambodia. Like Bangkok, they reject any compromise with Vietnam which, according to them, acts only as a proxy. When in 1979 the influx of boat people made the countries of ASEAN fear destabilization, Singapore declared that 'battle was already joined'. This analysis legitimizes a certain rapprochement with China, which aids the anti-Vietnamese resistance to sustain itself in Cambodia.[23] Singapore has several times suggested that ASEAN provide military aid to that resistance, but has met a blank Indonesian rejection on this issue. 'ASEAN's support for the Khmers Rouges has its limits. It is not ASEAN that is in conflict with Vietnam', the Indonesian Minister of Foreign Affairs said in 1982, 'the conflict is between Vietnam and China'.[24]

For Indonesia, like Malaysia, makes a very different analysis: China is the principal danger and Vietnam is capable of standing up to China, as it showed, in particular in March 1979. The perception of the Chinese danger rests on the risks of subversion linked to the communist parties (Djakarta attributes to Beijing a decisive role in the Indonesian crisis of 1965) and the Chinese minorities. Beijing's warlike policy towards Vietnam is deemed contrary to the interests of ASEAN which fears an uncontrollable spread of the conflict. Bangkok's pro-Chinese line appears worrying to Djakarta and Kuala Lumpur. Vietnam and the USSR thus touch a sensitive chord when they evoke the Chinese danger. The Soviet danger appears on the contrary to be less immediate.

Indonesia and Malaysia feel that coexistence with Vietnam is still possible. Suharto's Indonesia has succeeded in preserving good relations with Hanoi, while resisting the temptation to take part in the Vietnam war. The Indonesian generals are sensitive to the nationalism of the Vietnamese whose struggle evokes for them Indonesia's struggle against Dutch colonialism. Djakarta feels that Vietnam's present dependence on the USSR is purely conjunctural and that Hanoi, which is first and foremost defending its own interests, will get out of it as soon as it is able to. It is necessary, therefore, to give it the possibility of once again becoming faithful to its principles of independence.[25] The divergences between Hanoi and Moscow on several points (see Georges Boudarel's chapter) have not escaped the Indonesians or the Malaysians. While Singapore and Bangkok feel that a weakened Vietnam will be forced to make sacrifices, Djakarta and Kuala Lumpur think that prolongation of the conflict will serve only to deepen its dependence on the USSR, and, while Vietnam must not be too strong, neither must it be too weak and incapable of resisting China. The right course must, therefore, be to seek an understanding with Vietnam so as to find a balance in South-East Asia and limit the influence of the great powers there. Indonesia is all the more able to understand Vietnam's concern for security because it settled the problem of Timor itself through armed intervention and annexation. Although it falls in with ASEAN's calls for a Vietnamese withdrawal, it would doubtless be able to accept a Cambodia dominated by Vietnam without too much difficulty.

At the diplomatic level, ASEAN has had the Vietnamese presence in Cambodia condemned at the UN each year since 1979. In addition, the dialogue opened up with Vietnam has remained blocked.

In this context, the USSR has sometimes been seen as a guarantee against a possible Vietnamese aggression or as an agent of conciliation with Vietnam. When the China–Vietnam war of February–March 1979 had tightened links between Hanoi and Moscow, the USSR endeavoured to reassure General Kriangsak (March 1979) and then Hussein Onn (September 1979) about Vietnam's intentions. The tendency to conciliation then seemed to have the upper hand. Hanoi was manifesting a new interest in ZOPFAN while Indonesia and Malaysia were setting out the 'Kuantan principle' (March 1980) which made a settlement of the Indo-Chinese conflict dependent on a Vietnam freed of Soviet influence and also of the Chinese threat – which implied recognition of Vietnamese pre-eminence in Indo-China. The Vietnamese incursion into Thailand, in response to the unilateral repatriation of Khmer refugees, put a halt to these beginnings of a compromise and restored the unity of ASEAN, backed by the United States, Japan and China.

Yet, within ASEAN, the forces favourable to a dialogue with Vietnam have persisted. The USSR tries to encourage them, by actively supporting the offers of negotiation made by the countries of Indo-China proposing a regional conference on South-East Asia.[26] But ASEAN rejects these proposals since, as they see it, it is the Vietnamese presence in Cambodia that is the source of the problem and it is this that must be the subject of negotiations. In addition, it does not want to give the Phnom Penh government *de facto* recognition by sitting down with it at the negotiating table. Hanoi, for its part, rejects the international conference proposed by ASEAN on the Cambodia problem. The dialogue of the deaf continues.

For the advocates of compromise within ASEAN, the international conference in New York (July 1981) meeting in the absence of the USSR and Vietnam, ought above all to have been a positive stage in the search for a solution, by providing elements capable of reassuring Hanoi.[27] The determined opposition of China and the lack of support from the United States doomed this attempt and showed how small is ASEAN's room for manoeuvre.

Simultaneously, ASEAN, obliged to support the unpopular Khmers Rouges, endeavoured to moderate the support it gives them by adding to them the resistance movements led by Son Sann and Sihanouk. This diverse coalition finally came about only in June 1982 after Indonesia and Malaysia had threatened to terminate their support for the Khmers Rouges, which would have jeopardized their seat at the UN.

In the autumn of 1982, the Sino-Soviet rapprochement proposed by Leonid Brezhnev in March introduced a new element into the situation in the region. For, while Vietnam and China were very slightly softening their position on the withdrawal of Vietnamese forces, the USSR was renewing its assurances to Bangkok regarding Vietnam's intentions, while at the Non-Aligned Conference in New Delhi (March 1983) a new, more promising, proposal for dialogue seemed to be emerging.

Almost at once a new stiffening became apparent while the Vietnamese offensive against the Khmers Rouges led to armed clashes on the Thai border. Bangkok and Singapore made statements hostile to the USSR, which warned ASEAN against continuing to aid the Khmer resistance. In April 1983, China saw fit to give a new armed warning to Vietnam.

Yet the tendency to détente seems likely to persist. Vietnam has carried out other troop withdrawals. Conversations are continuing and it may be that this is no longer altogether a dialogue of the deaf, even if the evolution is extremely slow.

Mr Gorbachev's accession to power in 1985 appears to have reinforced both the trend to openness and the possibility of an increased Soviet role in Asia and the Pacific. His speech in Vladivostok, on 28 July 1986, made this abundantly clear. The visit to Thailand by Mr E. Shevardnaze, the Soviet Minister of Foreign Affairs, was intended to reassure his hosts and underlines the point.[27] But when the USSR sought to reinforce its influence in the South Pacific islands, this new policy, actively supportive of a denuclearized zone in South-East Asia (a notion which Washington opposes) did not evoke a response from the ASEAN countries. They were disappointed that Moscow did not seem disposed to pressure Hanoi into a settlement of the Cambodian problem and was content to reiterate the proposals put forward by the Vietnamese. Caution remains the rule.

*   *   *

While the ASEAN countries are decided upon maintaining their unity at all costs, for without it their international significance would be greatly reduced, it remains that the Association covers two opposed tendencies that sometimes find it hard to coexist.

For Thailand and Singapore, the Soviet danger incarnated by Vietnam justifies an alignment on the Chinese and American positions. It is still too soon to assess the consequences of the Chinese shift on this point. In Thailand, the situation remains fluid and voices, like Kriangsak's, are being raised in favour of a political solution to the conflict. For Indonesia and Malaysia – even though their positions do not always coincide – there is no question of letting themselves become involved in the Cold War logic that underlies the Vietnamese conflict. The Filipinos adopt a more reserved attitude.

The Soviet danger is not perceived as immediate and the aim remains to achieve a regional balance in South-East Asia that would enable Indo-China and ASEAN to coexist in peace. It is to this end that Indonesia has developed the theme of a necessary (and problematical) self-reliance on the part of the countries of ASEAN, which should above all find in themselves the resources to make it possible to resist the communist danger, since the imperatives of the great powers do not always correspond to the interests of weaker countries.

On the world level, Singapore is the only member of ASEAN to develop explicitly the theme of the USSR as a global threat. The others, being more moderate, also feel the danger of the USSR, a communist great power, but they seem to admit that coexistence remains possible, provided that limits are put on its influence. To the extent that the United States is the only country capable of counter-balancing Soviet power on a world scale, the pugnacity of the Reagan administration, which put an end to the hesitant policy of the Carter years, has rather reassured them, even if it is also a source of irritations. They, nevertheless, do not intend to let themselves be dragged into a situation where they could no longer be in control of deciding what is good for them.

Notes

1. A few statistics: Indonesia: 1,900,000 km², 170 million inhabitants; Thailand: 514,000 km², 53 million inhabitants; Malaysia: 335,000 km², 16 million inhabitants; Philippines: 297,000 km², 57 million inhabitants; Singapore: 581 km², 2,600,000 inhabitants.

2. See the Kuala Lumpur declaration (27 November 1971) in *Indonesia Quarterly*, IV, 1,2,3,4, 1976, pp. 108–9. Since 1976 the English abbreviation ZOPFAN has usually been used to express the concept of a 'Zone of Peace, Freedom and Neutrality' by the countries concerned.

3. ASEAN has no military content, but some of its members are linked by bilateral military cooperation agreements.

4. *Le Monde*, 16 October and 29 December 1982.

5. Ibid., 17 May 1983.

6. See Shee Poon Kim, 'Insurgency in Southeast Asia', *Problems of Communism*, May–June 1983, pp. 45–55.

7. In this connection mention might be made of a survey made in Indonesia: 28% of those asked about external dangers mentioned China first, 23% the Soviet Union, 21% Vietnam, 11% the United States, 8% Japan. On domestic dangers, in first place were corruption and misuse of power (44%), the communists (22%), fundamentalist Islam having only 4%. *Asiaweek*, 5 September 1980, p. 17.

8. We should recall the debate over the proposal for a second Bandung conference as to whether the USSR was or was not an Asian power, as it asserted in order to participate in it. Again, when in 1956 Sukarno had proposed measures against multi-partyism, it should be noted that he had been impressed by his recent visit to the USSR and China. Looking back a little earlier, the positive role of the USSR at the time when Indonesia was fighting for its independence should be remembered, while noting that diplomatic recognition came only in January 1950, and the exchange of ambassadors in 1954. In its time the October revolution had had a great impact in the Dutch East Indies where the first communist party in Asia was formed in 1920.

9. 'Asian collective security: the Soviet view', by H. M. Hensel, *Orbis*, 19, 4, Winter 1976, pp. 1564–80 and 'The Soviet Union and Southeast Asia: interests, goals and constraints' by S. W. Simon, *Orbis*, 25, 1, Spring 1981, pp. 53–88.

10. See Lee Poh'Ping, 'Malaysian view of Southeast Asia', *Asian Survey*, XXII, 6, June 1982, p. 520.

11. S. W. Simon, 'The Soviet Union and Southeast Asia', op. cit., quotes the following figures: trade with the USSR and Eastern Europe as a percentage of total trade (in 1978): 1.1% for Indonesia; 0.4% for Malaysia; 0.2% for the Philippines; 0.5% for Singapore; 1% for Thailand.

12. See *Far Eastern Economic Review*, 7 September 1979. One Indonesian judged Soviet products thus: 'Besides, we know the technical limitations of the Russians. They are very good in some fields but a flop in others. They produce good steel but they are behind in computers. We must look very carefully at what they can offer.' *Asia Yearbook*, 1977, p. 192.

13. Quoted by L. Buszynski, 'Thailand: the erosion of a balanced foreign policy', *Asian Survey*, XXII, 11, November 1982, p. 1041. Similarly, the Minister of Foreign Affairs in the previous government felt that the USSR could 'contribute to the stability of Southeast Asia'.

14. The Secretary-General of the Thai National Security Council, Prasong

Soonsiri, counted 15 warships there, including submarines, and reconnaissance aircraft and mentioned special facilities at Cam Ranh (floating drydock and electronic monitoring station), *Far Eastern Economic Review*, 11 August 1983.

15. M. Ghazali Shafie, in *Far Eastern Economic Review*, 30 October 1981, p. 34 and *Asiaweek*, 14 August 1981, p. 12.

16. J. Wanandi, 'Conflict and cooperation in the Asia–Pacific region: an Indonesian perspective', *Asian Survey*, June 1982, p. 513.

17. See *Far Eastern Economic Review*, 2 June 1983.

18. Ibid., 6 January 1983.

19. See *Asiaweek*, 20 June 1981.

20. See *Far Eastern Economic Review*, 6 August 1976, p. 52.

21. The expression comes from Singapore which also describes Vietnam as the 'Cuba of Asia'. Thailand has spoken in this connection of a 'Trojan horse'.

22. *Kompas*, 19 January 1980. On the Thai position concerning the 'global dimension' of the conflict, see also the statements by the Minister of Foreign Affairs, Air Chief Marshal Siddhi Savetsila, to the World Balance of Power Conference (July 1983, Great Britain), quoted in *Thailand News and Information*, 40, July 1983.

23. Singapore has no diplomatic relations with China, which does not prevent quite frequent exchanges of visits. Lee Kuan Yew went to Beijing in 1976 and November 1980, Deng Xiao Ping came in November 1976 and Zhao Ziyang in August 1981.

24. *Kompas*, 22 February 1982.

25. *Suara Karya*, 6 March 1980.

26. See L. Buszynski, op. cit., *Asian Survey*, May 1981, pp. 548–49.

27. Recognition of Vietnam's security problems, provision of economic aid, disarmament of the Khmers Rouges after the withdrawal of 'foreign forces', elections supervised by the UN.

5 The USSR as seen by Vietnamese Communists

Georges Boudarel

For many years, Vietnam was perceived both by the Vietnamese communists and by their most determined opponents as the key centre of the confrontation between the socialist camp headed by the USSR and a free world aligned behind the United States. But, quite clearly, this Manichaean ideological view could not fully account for a complex situation in which determinants deriving from Vietnamese society itself played a considerable role. In the analysis of Vietnam's relations with the USSR, for example, the problems posed by the north–south cleavage, the ethnic and religious diversity of the country, the high density of the Vietnamese population and its extreme poverty, are all just as important as strictly diplomatic considerations.

Terra incognita . . . or utopia

The USSR had the initial advantage of not having played any part in Vietnamese history. Unlike China which, for several millennia, maintained very close relations with its neighbour to the south, Russia was, until the early 1920s, totally unknown to Vietnam. Before that date, relations between the two countries were virtually non-existent. They were limited to the contacts which a number of intellectuals, hostile to French colonial rule, had maintained with the Russian legation. In 1884, the senior resident in Annam informed the Court of Hué of Russia's 'good offices' in favour of an agreement on Tonkin between France and the Manchu dynasty.[1] Almost ten years later, the Russian plenipotentiary in Beijing informed his French counterpart that he had been contacted by Annamites claiming to be secret envoys from the Court of Hué. Subsequently, during the Boxer War, these same individuals again attempted to make contact with the Russians.[2] The modernist intellectuals, who initiated agitation in the centre of the country in 1905, went all the way to Cam Ranh to see the Russian fleet that had moored there. A few weeks later, when they learned of the Russian defeat at Tsushima, Russia lost its attractiveness and was forgotten.

This absence of historical depth in Russian-Vietnamese relations was, however, paradoxically to favour the nationalist movement's infatuation with Soviet Russia after the 1920s. *Terra incognita* was to become utopia for the revolutionary movements. Russia was not judged for what it really was, but in terms of its enormous potential and its capacity to come to the aid of the forces of national liberation. This attractiveness was certainly reinforced by the absence of any bilateral dispute – or common border – which enabled Vietnam to judge that it would be able to retain its independence in the event of any possible pressure. Subsequently, the alliance with the USSR was motivated by the need to have a counterweight to China, following a tradition of geopolitical balance going back to the early 15th Century.[3]

Basing themselves on the pattern of Bolshevik organization, the Vietnamese communists succeeded in exercising their political hegemony over the whole country, despite the harsh repression used against them. They even succeeded, thanks to effective propaganda, in discrediting their nationalist rivals, presented as 'tools of the foreigner'. This discrediting of the traditional nationalist parties influenced Vietnamese opinion to the point that it became 'a seal of infamy very difficult to remove'.[4] Thus, by brandishing the national flag after 1940 and refraining from referring to the class struggle, Ho Chi Minh succeeded in cementing national unity around him and proclaiming the independence of the country in 1945. At that stage of the national liberation struggle, Soviet–Vietnamese relations remained limited. If we are to believe Major Patti, an American secret service agent and a friend of Ho Chi Minh, the Soviet representative in Hanoi was mainly concerned with ensuring the safe repatriation of Soviet citizens.[5] But in the eyes of the Vietnamese communists the USSR still remained a country beyond all suspicion, whose intentions could not be doubted.

The ups and downs of an 'indestructible friendship'

After his arrival in power, Mao Zedong lost no time in recognizing the Democratic Republic of Vietnam, and pressed Moscow to do the same. Already at this time, relations between the CPSU and CPC were beginning to become strained, according to the representative of the Comintern in Yenan.[6] But, on the question of Vietnam, the positions of the two countries were still largely identical. Moscow let all its aid to Hanoi pass through Beijing. As for the political and technical advisers sent to Vietnam, they were all Chinese. The Vietnamese leadership, which had reservations in 1954 on the idea of a ceasefire negotiated in Geneva, came round in the end to the opinion of its two big allies which, at that time, wanted to make concessions to the West in order to promote peaceful coexistence.[7] Totally confident in the solidity of the socialist camp and the support that it would not fail to give them subsequently on all levels, the rulers in Hanoi accepted Zhou en Lai's plan in 1954, envisaging a separate settlement of the three Indo-Chinese problems (Cambodia, Laos, Vietnam), as well as the temporary partition of the last two.[8] Although the Vietnamese Communist Party's leadership today seems to criticize China for having conceived that plan with the sole purpose of doing it harm, there is nothing to prove that it had any such feeling at the time. At the San Francisco conference in September 1951, it had, moreover, even accepted without recriminations Soviet support for Chinese claims to the Paracels and Nancha islands.

Until the late 1950s, the policy of the USSR and the other socialist countries was analysed in Hanoi globally, in the name of essentially ideological considerations. The idyllic image of the socialist countries was then so strong that it was peddled in laudatory naive doggerel in praise of the two Big Brothers. The historic animosity between Vietnam and China was erased and replaced by the image of a community linking the USSR, China and Vietnam under the leadership of Stalin, Mao Zedong and Ho Chi Minh. This friendship was hailed day in day out on the radio and broadcast in every village thanks to a network of loudspeakers installed with Soviet aid.

This triangular relationship began to unravel under the twin effect of the China–Vietnam conflict and destalinization. The Vietnamese leadership never agreed to draw the consequences of the Khruschev report to the attention of the 20th Congress. Not only did it conflict with its Stalinist and Confucian convictions, but in addition it hampered its action to reunify the country. And this mistrust was hardly attenuated when, in 1957, Moscow proposed the simultaneous admission to the UN of the two Vietnams and the two Koreas.

Now seeing the USSR as a country eaten away by Khruschevian revisionism, the Vietnamese leadership embarked on a policy of balancing its relations with Beijing, despite the reservations of Ho Chi Minh and the hostility of General Giap. Hanoi then ceased presenting the USSR as 'the leader of the socialist camp'. By the early 1960s it simply described it as the 'centre of the socialist camp'. At the end of the Khruschev period, relations between the USSR and Vietnam reached their lowest level. During the central committee session of December 1963–January 1964, which the Vietnamese press reported only very partially, revisionism was denounced in terms identical to those used by Beijing, even if the USSR was not mentioned by name.

But, with the beginning of the American escalation in Vietnam, Hanoi had to put an end to its doctrinal rigidity and demonstrate a greater realism. With China sinking into the cultural revolution, the Vietnamese leaders had no choice but to tighten their alliance with Moscow so as to face up to the American war machine. Even if the passionate love affair was over, it had given way to a marriage of reason: it was not without its stormy moments and family scenes; these were settled behind closed doors, but echoes of what was happening sometimes reached the outside world. Thus in 1967, in what is generally called the 'Hoang Minh Chinh affair', important party cadres, including the head of the Party School, were placed under house arrest for spying for the USSR. To forestall such activities, the National Assembly passed a 'law on the repression of counter-revolutionary crimes'. This law, which was undoubtedly aimed at the intelligence services of the socialist countries, laid down different penalties for the crimes of 'treason', 'subversion' or 'fleeing abroad'.[9] This affair, which was made public only in 1968,[10] had, however, been reported to American intelligence agencies by North Vietnamese prisoners and deserters at the time of the Tet offensive.

But Hanoi's resentment of Moscow reached its height in 1972, with President Nixon's visit to Moscow. It even surfaced in the press, and notably in the daily *Nhan Zan* which denounced the 'narrow national interests' of the USSR, and also those of China. The revolution, it stated, 'is bestrewn with flowers and perfumed, opportunism is a stinking mire'. A poem by Che Lan Vien, published at about the same time, was even more explicit: 'Learned friends . . . who have explored space . . . A waste of time. All will be lost if imperialism is not defeated.'[11] During the winter of 1974–75, when war preparations to reconquer the south were under discussion in Hanoi, General Van Tien Zung invoked the shortage of munitions to reject the launching of large-scale operations. It took the insistence of General Tran Van Tra, backed by Pham Hung, representing the political bureau in the South, for the attack against Phuoc Long to be launched. This battle, which rapidly gave the communists control of a whole province, constituted the 'divine surprise' which totally transformed the initial operational plans. The book published by General Tran Van Tra in March 1982, but quickly withdrawn from bookshops, testifies to the great independence that Hanoi demonstrated with regard to its Soviet ally.[12] It would probably not be going too far to judge that the 1975 campaign was conceived and led by Hanoi despite the reservations or even opposition of Moscow. This Vietnamese autonomy of action was demonstrated three years later, at the time of the invasion of Cambodia. Although occurring shortly after the signing of the Soviet–Vietnamese treaty, it is unlikely that the decision to intervene was taken in Moscow. In that case, it may even be thought that the USSR was opposed to it, reading the communiqué put out by the conference of the Warsaw Pact countries held shortly before the Vietnamese invasion:

> The participants did not even, as was expected, express their support for Vietnam, a member of COMECON, which had just signed a treaty of friendship and cooperation with Moscow, whereas it mentioned the efforts made by North Korea for reunification.[13]

Moreover, traces of disagreements between the Soviets and the Vietnamese about Cambodia before the invasion can be found at the time of the discussion of the affair before the Human Rights sub-commission in Geneva in the autumn of 1978. Whereas, by then, Hanoi had already taken the decision to get rid of Pol Pot, the Soviet government felt itself obliged to continue to defend the Phnom Penh regime. Refuting the overwhelming documentary evidence of the violation of human rights in Cambodia, the Soviet delegate denied their veracity on the pretext that they emanated from political refugees who were 'mostly traitors, people who put about lies to recover the positions they have lost'. 'All revolutions', he added, 'have their victims, the problem is to know whether a country has the right to choose its own political, social and economic regime.'[14]

Despite the Vietnamese military success in Cambodia, the divergences of view between the Soviets and the Vietnamese on the question were not totally removed. They were expressed in December 1981 at the time of the Pen Sovan affair. And it can be said with confidence that the resumption of the dialogue between Moscow and Beijing worries Hanoi.

Thus, since 1965, the Vietnamese communists' view of the USSR has come out of its strictly ideological framework and become integrated into a geostrategic military context, in which state interests are supreme, even though these are integrated into the theoretical matrix of Marxism–Leninism.

But if one looks behind the official façade of unanimity, it is clear that the

Vietnamese communists have always been divided on the question of the USSR. In a letter addressed to the National Assembly in June 1981, Doctor Nguyen Khac Vien, who declared himself a firm supporter of the alliance with the USSR, criticized: 'people with "a narrow nationalist outlook" who "want to play two even three sides", and who harbour the illusion that the imperialists will help us if we move away from the Soviet bloc.'[15]

Even though this tendency appears to be a minority one, and even though the Fifth Congress of the Vietnamese Communist Party was marked by the victory of the upholders of doctrinal orthodoxy, this simple letter is there to prove the existence of a more pragmatic tendency, the importance of which may develop, as a result of the Sino-Soviet rapprochement.

Despite partly contradictory objectives, the interests of the USSR and Vietnam appear to be strategically convergent. Use of Cam Ranh Bay and the port of Da Nang, situated opposite the American bases in the Philippines, is of vital strategic importance and well worth sacrifices. For its part, Vietnam has cruel need of Soviet military assistance; and yet it still remains the case that at the regional level, the two countries have different preoccupations. Seared by its experience in the 1950s, when it left Beijing to monopolize aid to Vietnam, the USSR today wants to avoid having its aid to Cambodia and Laos pass through Hanoi. The special relationship that Hanoi has with Phnom Penh and Vientiane is perceived in Moscow as harmful to the USSR's direct influence.

While continuation of hostilities in the Indo-Chinese peninsula cannot fail to strengthen Soviet–Vietnamese relations, and hence deepen Hanoi's military dependence, the Sino-Soviet rapprochement may paradoxically give Vietnam more room to manoeuvre.

This diplomatic 'big game' between the two principal communist powers may well put an end to the Cambodian crisis which Soviet policy has exploited, although it did not provoke it.

The Cambodian litmus test

The whole current tragedy of South-East Asia goes back to the late 1960s when a handful of Cambodian communists embarked on building up an ultra-revolutionary party. From the very beginning they cut themselves off from all potential allies, beginning with the Vietnamese communists, whom they accused of having sold out 'the interests of the Khmer revolution' at Geneva in 1954, whereas in reality the initiative for international negotiations had come from Beijing. And whereas the Vietnamese Communist Party abandoned ideas of using Maoist methods in domestic policy as early as 1954, while moving closer to Beijing diplomatically, the Pol Pot–Yeng Sary–Son Sen groups which took to the maquis in 1963 became increasingly radicalized. In 1965, a Khmers Rouges delegation had stormy discussions with Vietnamese leaders who were pressing them to moderation in dealing with Sihanouk. In 1967, when the Cultural Revolution was at its height in China, the Cambodian communists aligned themselves with the positions of the Chinese ultra-left. They also took advantage of this revolutionary context to step up their military action against the regime of Prince Sihanouk without, however, succeeding in destabilizing it. But they put the South Vietnamese revolutionaries, holed up in the Cambodian sanctuary, in a difficult situation. These divergences between the Vietnamese and Cambodians were somewhat papered over in March 1970 following General Lon Nol's *coup de force*. But it was very difficult to translate the proclaimed unity of action into reality on the ground. During the summer of 1972, while the Vietnamese communist forces were withdrawing from the right bank of the Mekong in order to facilitate the signing of an agreement with the United States, the Khmers Rouges were engaging in what amounted to an extermination of 'undesirable elements' who were natives of Cambodia, China and Vietnam. The field survey carried out by K. MacQuinn between 1972 and 1974 details the terrifying cruelty they resorted to.[16] This ill-conceived policy led, immediately the Second Indo-China War ended, in April 1975, to the launching by the Khmers Rouges of hostilities all along the border with South Vietnam.

For a number of both ideological and political reasons, the Vietnamese communists kept quiet about all these excesses for over three years. Only in 1978 did they decide to go public about them, just before launching a lightning attack to which the Chinese tried to react through a massive unexpected attack on Vietnam. Just when the Tanzanian intervention in Uganda was putting an end to the regime of Idi Amin Dada, to the general relief of international opinion, the Vietnamese intervention was producing the opposite effect. Its initial silence on the crimes of the Pol Pot regime, suddenly broken by a violent campaign of denunciation, lost Hanoi all credibility. In addition, it was difficult for its invocation of grand humanitarian principles in Cambodia to be convincing – at a time when the exodus of boat people was just getting under way in South Vietnam. Thus, rather paradoxically, China's support for Pol Pot, and its aggression against Vietnam, provoked less criticism than the Vietnamese intervention, which was yet generally welcomed with relief by the Khmer population. But by asserting that the situation created by its intervention was irreversible and closing the door on any political solution that might lead to the re-emergence of a non-aligned Cambodia, the disarmament of the Khmers Rouges and the return of the refugees, Hanoi soon lost the benefit of what it had done. Its action, which definitely had its humanitarian side, soon took on the form of a policy of hegemony.

By deciding to launch a war of attrition against Hanoi, Beijing finally succeeded in pushing into Moscow's arms a communist Vietnam betrayed by its former ally and now haunted by the spectre of the 'hereditary enemy'. Excessively overstretched and with poor means of transport and communications to assure its defence on several fronts, Vietnam cannot feel itself secure when China manifests open hostility towards it and sets both its western neighbours against it. Behind the Pol Pot group, which actually set off the new crisis, could be seen the immense shadow of China. Beijing's support for the Khmers Rouges eventually became the prime justification for Vietnamese action in Cambodia; and the evolution of Sino-American relations in the 1970s could only aggravate Vietnamese worries.

In order to avoid encirclement, Vietnamese diplomacy had attempted to win over the ASEAN countries towards which China had made an opening in 1972, by supporting Indonesia's and Malaysia's stand on the non-international character of the waters in the Strait of Malacca and taking up the idea of ZOPFAN (Zone of Peace, Freedom and Neutrality) adopted by the Kuala Lumpur conference of 1971. This campaign of seduction obliged the Soviet Union to embark on a rapprochement with the ASEAN countries while continuing to show a degree of prudence. For its part, Hanoi had at first remained deaf to proposals made to the three countries of Indo-China to join ASEAN. In February 1976, at a time when Soviet and Chinese reactions to the ASEAN summit were measured and cautious, the theoretical journal of the Vietnamese Communist Party called on ASEAN to choose between two paths, one of which was seen as leading inevitably to defeat. For its part, the army newspaper accused Indonesia of making itself the tool of American strategy.[17] Subsequently, the Vietnamese position became more flexible, with the Deputy Minister of Foreign Affairs Phan Hien's visit to South-East Asia in the early summer of 1976. Between 1976 and 1978, Hanoi made a number of friendly gestures and continued to do so until the intervention in Cambodia put an end to détente in the region.

Today, the settlement of the Cambodian question seems to depend largely on the evolution of Sino-Soviet relations. Beijing, which seems to make this problem a test of Soviet 'goodwill', is believed to have suggested a settlement plan to Moscow in January 1983. For its part the Phnom Penh government made a gesture by receiving for the first time a delegation of American personalities led by former Ambassador E. Swank.[18] Not to be left behind, Yuri Andropov informed the Thai Prime Minister, in March 1983, that his country was ready to favour 'negotiations aimed at settling regional problems by political means'.[19] France, anxious to save Vietnam from having 'an increasingly exclusive tête-à-tête with its Soviet ally',[20] sent its Minister of Foreign Affairs to Hanoi. But while feeling that it would be 'unreasonable' to exclude Vietnam from a settlement in Cambodia, France, speaking through François Mitterand, specified that it 'does not recognize, and will not recognize' the government established in Phnom Penh and that no solution could be found without the withdrawal of 'foreign forces that are enslaving Cambodia'.

Faced with the prospect of a normalization of Sino-Soviet relations, Vietnam seems to have been caught short. And when Le Zuan went to Moscow to meet Leonid Brezhnev, Truong Chinh denounced 'the intrigues of Chinese expansionists and hegemonists'.[21] At the beginning of May 1983, Vietnam nevertheless made its second partial troop withdrawal from Cambodia, for the first time summoning the international press to verify, on the spot, that its decision was indeed being implemented. In June, at his meeting with his Thai counterpart, the Vietnamese Minister of Foreign Affairs declared himself in favour of an 'independent, neutral and non-aligned Cambodia'.

Although this formula lends itself to several interpretations, the fact that the Thai minister expressed his willingness to visit Hanoi 'in due course' and that Vietnam expressed its intention of not imposing recognition of the *fait accompli* in Cambodia on its neighbours, indicates a slow evolution of the situation.[22]

A new version of the Great Leap Forward
The striking victory won at Saigon in April 1975 gave rise to the illusion within the

Vietnamese ruling group that everything was possible through voluntarism and a high degree of mobilization based on a pervasive apparatus of repression. Thus there emerged:

> the idea of a rapid leap in the economy: ill-thought out investment in numerous sectors of heavy industry, ill-considered increases in the size of cooperatives in the North, accelerated collectivization in the South and the removal of villages as in Nghi Tinh.[23]

Advance rapidly, advance forcefully: such was the new slogan. In the north of the country a more ambitious plan to rebuild the countryside endeavoured to transform the district headquarter towns into 'agro-towns' centralizing all agricultural production. According to a plan for bureaucratic and technological centralization based on the Soviet model, Vietnam was embarking on a 'Great Leap Forward' which is precisely what it had avoided launching in the late 1950s. Thanks to Moscow's material and human support, this policy envisaged a massive movement of people from the north to the war-devastated south. But lack of proper allocation of resources soon meant that each region, each province, each district wanted to be a self-sufficient entity:

> not to mention those who dreamed of making atomic weapons. On such a path the country is heading straight for disaster. The example of the Chinese Great Leap Forward is staring us in the face.[24]

It was not long before this policy ran into trouble. It ended up with an unprecedented economic crisis and shortages. Soviet aid, previously so effective during the war, proved incapable of solving the problems posed by nationalization and accelerated collectivization. Furthermore, it seemed not to reflect the management capacities of the cadres nor the aspirations of the population, including that of the guerrilla zones in the south previously held by the communists. The rapid abandonment of the political programme of the PRG (Provisional Revolutionary Government) which envisaged a slow move towards unification, a pluralist political system and a market economy, provoked disillusionment and passive resistance.

Soviet aid, ill-adapted to the circumstances of reconstruction, turned out to be also extremely parsimonious. As a result of domestic economic difficulties, Moscow was obliged to reduce its deliveries of food products. For the European socialist bloc as a whole, they fell from 1.4 million tons in 1978 to 0.8 million tons two years later.[25] In fact, the socialist bloc proved incapable of solving the problems raised by the importation of its own methods. Furthermore, in the key sectors of the development of Vietnam (tropical agronomy, off-shore drilling) its skills were limited.

The financial terms of Soviet loans turned out to be as draconian as those of Western loans, and more restrictive: 'We are caught up in the Soviet economic orbit . . . and our "friends" conduct their commercial policy sharply. They are tough in business and don't make presents.'[26]

The aid initially planned by the USSR seems to have been cut by 40%, because of its economic difficulties. It appears, too, to have raised the price of its oil and demanded a greater and greater share in the management of the Vietnamese economy which it deemed to be badly run. The Vietnamese seem to have replied to these demands by restricting the freedom of movement of Soviet advisers and subjecting Soviet warships using the base at Cam Ranh to endless checks.[27] At the beginning of 1981, the chairman of the state planning commission and the officials in charge of ideological problems, who had complained in veiled terms of Soviet pressures, received a reprimand and thus failed to get into the Political Bureau.[28]

The difficulties encountered in cooperation with the USSR gave rise to an intense debate within the Vietnamese political leadership. This seems to have ended in the autumn of 1979 in the partial victory of the supporters of a moderate line. In fact, the 6th resolution of the Central Committee advocated a more realistic, more flexible and more decentralized management. It also granted more room for individual initiative, material incentives and the private sector. These responses had the effect of favouring increased agricultural production. In 1982, the paddy rice harvest was 8% higher than that of the previous year. For the first time since 1975, the plan targets in agriculture were achieved and even largely surpassed.

But this political shift did not indicate any real change of camp. After two years of internal debates, the 5th Congress of the VCP, meeting in March 1982, left economic problems pending, even giving a slight advantage to the supporters of orthodoxy. The fervent Maoists of the 1950s, reconverted to a pro-Sovietism that was more formal than real, retained their positions, although the supporters of a more flexible line, better adapted to the internal and external conjuncture, were not removed.

Torn between the Soviet model and the Chinese or even Hungarian experiences, the Vietnamese leadership continues today to seek its path. Frightened by the sudden resurgence of the private sector, it adopted a series of measures in April 1983 aimed at stifling it. Once again, bureaucratic complications limited the small room for manoeuvre that departments, enterprises and individuals had recently come to enjoy. After a phase of slight liberalization, the pendulum seems to have swung back towards *dirigisme*, centralization and coercion.

These numerous hesitations show clearly that the belief in the USSR as the ideal model, the home of ready-made solutions and dispenser of generous and disinterested aid, had considerably weakened. But to the extent that the reference to the USSR legitimizes the established government, it would seem to be difficult and dangerous for it to be officially questioned.

In the 1950s and 1960s, China and the USSR served as examples for Vietnam. With the advent of Khruschev, only the reference to China continued to exist, the USSR being considered as deviationist and revisionist. Faced with the necessities of the war against the United States, Vietnam was constrained to move closer to the USSR. Soviet aid, despite its inadequacies, nevertheless played an essential role in the victory. This assistance, combined with a Leninist-type organization and mobilization around patriotic and social slogans, contributed to forging an instrument of an extraordinary operational value.

But following the war, the use of the same instruments resulted in failure. At the very time when Vietnam could judge bitterly the parsimonious and not necessarily effective character of Soviet aid, however, the necessities of the war with China led it once again to move closer to Moscow. But the terms of this alliance are decidedly different in character from that which presided over Soviet–Vietnamese relations in the 1960s. Hanoi finds in Soviet military equipment and deliveries of fuel the indispensable means for maintaining its presence in Cambodia. For its part, the USSR sees in the port of Cam Ranh a particularly valuable strategic facility for its Pacific fleet. Despite its purely instrumental character, this new alliance will, eventually, suffer from the disillusionment of public opinion with the Soviet model. If Soviet aid contributed to the victory of the Vietnamese communists, it has not been of great help to them in winning the battle of economic reconstruction.

Without formally modifying the Soviet–Vietnamese alliance, Gorbachev has, in recent years, set up a dynamic which changes the overall context. The improvement of Sino-Soviet relations has aroused great anxiety amongst the orthodox communists of Hanoi, especially as it is part of a general policy of greater openness towards ASEAN, which remains keen to see a political settlement in Cambodia. On the other hand, the more pragmatic Vietnamese leaders see this development as a reason to hope that their country may eventually emerge from its isolation. In Cambodia, the Vietnamese military success in clearing the bases of the Khmers Rouges and of the nationalists led by Sihanouk and Son San remains a Pyrrhic victory, since China maintains supplies of munitions and credits to the insurgents, with the connivance of Bangkok.

In Vietnam itself, the economic crisis resulting from the accumulated errors of the ideologues has attracted Soviet criticisms and led to considerable discontent, even within the Communist Party itself. In late 1986, during the VIth Congress of the Vietnamese Communist Party, reformers gained the upper hand, although they did not secure a decisive victory. Both the final resolution and the composition of the Political Bureau are evidence of a compromise, which doubtless does not correspond to Moscow's preferences in the matter. No new initiatives emerged on the diplomatic level. Whilst there is some evolution in the economy, the strategic deadlock continues, or at least so it seems. In fact, however, since Gorbachev's speech in Vladivostok on 28 July 1986, the situation in communist Asia has changed considerably. In January 1987, 'just as Mr Gorbachev confirmed the withdrawal of some of the Soviet troops in the Popular Republic of Mongolia, Ulan Bator and Washington announced the establishment of diplomatic relations'.[29] The USA had been active once again in Laos ever since autumn 1985.

An underlying Soviet influence is clearly at work in setting up this new international context, although to what extent this is the result of deliberate policy is more difficult to say. In any case, President Reagan's decision on 17 Feburary 1987 to send General John Vessey to Hanoi to pursue the quest for the bodies of M.I.A. American troops is one indubitable result. The journey was decided upon following a study, drawn up at the request of the White House, by Department of Defence and State Department officials, which concluded that 'In view of Hanoi's anxiety at the improvement of Sino-Soviet relations, and Hanoi's own desire to liberalize its economy, the time may have come for the US to normalize relations with Vietnam'.[30]

Everything considered, this outcome of Soviet policy is not as paradoxical as it seems at first. Since 1950, the USSR has always faithfully supported communist

Vietnam in its wars, without, however, wishing to see nothing but military victories as the outcome. The search for a compromise in Indo-China was always as much a constant of Soviet policy as was the supply of arms.

Notes

1. *Dai Nam Thuc Luc* (True writing on Dai Nam), Hanoi, Social Sciences Committee Publishing House, 1976, p. 174.

2. G. Coulet, *Les sociétés secrètes en terre d'Annam*, Saigon, Imprimerie C. Ardin, 1926, p. 308.

3. See Wang Gungwu, 'China and South-East Asia 1402–1424', in J. Ch'en and N. Starling (eds), *South-East Asia*, Cambridge, Cambridge University Press, 1970.

4. J. Verdès-Leroux, *Au service du parti. Le parti communiste, les intellectuels et la culture, 1944–1956*, Paris, Fayard-Minuit, 1983, p. 51.

5. A. Patti, *Why Vietnam? Prelude to America's Albatross*, Berkeley, University of California Press, 1980, pp. 178–81.

6. Van Phong, 'A la lecture du journal de Yenan'', *Nghiên Cun Lich Su*, 195, November–December 1980, pp. 88–90. Extracts reprinted in *Le Nouvel Observateur*, 17 June 1974.

7. *Beijing Information*, 10 December 1979.

8. B. Ponomarev, A. Gromyko, V. Khostov (eds), *Histoire de la politique de l'URSS 1945–1970*, Moscow, Progress Publishers, 1974, p. 194.

9. *Hoc Tâp*, 4, 1968, pp. 71–5.

10. Ibid.

11. Quotations reprinted in *Le Monde*, 24–25 April 1983.

12. Tran Van Tra, *Kêt thuc cuôc chiên tranh 30 nam* (The conclusion of a thirty-year war), Van Nghê, Ho Chi Minh City, 1982. Major extracts translated into French in G. Boudarel (texts collected by), *La bureaucratie au Viêt-nam*, Paris, L'Harmattan, 1983, pp. 173–221.

13. *Le Monde*, 25 November 1978.

14. Ibid., 17–18 September 1978.

15. Extracts from this letter were reprinted by P. Quinn-Judge in *Far Eastern Economic Review*, 26 February 1982, pp. 15–16.

16. See K. MacQuinn, 'Political change in war time. The Khmer revolution in Southern Cambodia – 1970–1974', *Naval War College Review*, Spring 1976, pp. 3–32.

17. Quoted in J. M. Van der Kroef, 'Hanoi and ASEAN: a new confrontation in Southeast Asia', *Asia Quarterly*, 1976/4, p. 257.

18. E. Swank, 'The land between Cambodia. Ten years later', *Indochina Issues*, April 1983.

19. *Le Monde*, 10 February 1983.

20. Ibid., 29 March 1983.

21. Ibid., 10–11 October 1983.

22. Libération, 11–12 June 1983.

23. Letter from Nguyen Khac Viên to the National Assembly in G. Boudarel, *La bureaucratie au Vietnam*, op. cit., p. 116 (see *Vietnam Courier*, 18, 6, 1982, p. 157).

24. Ibid., p. 117.

25. *Croissance des jeunes nations*, December 1981, p. 15.

26. *Le Point*, 2 May 1981.

27. Ibid.

28. See N. Chanda, 'Bickering begins as old friends fall out', *Far Eastern Economic Review*, 27 February 1981, pp. 32–33; 'Change of tune', Ibid., 12 June 1981, p. 7.

29. Richard Nations, 'La Mongolie joue ses atouts dans le grand jeu asiatique', *Le Monde Diplomatique*, April 1987, pp. 14–15.

30. Nayan Chanda, 'Reagan's Man to Hanoi', *Far Eastern Economic Review*, 30 April 1987, p. 13.

6 The USSR as seen by India

Max Zins

Relations between India and the Soviet Union have been a major component of the balance of power in South-East Asia since 1947. For two decades now, the two countries have maintained relations of 'peace, friendship and cooperation' that are remarkable for their closeness and longevity, as well as for their impact on the whole region. There is probably no other example of such long-lasting relations between the leading socialist country and a Third World country of India's stature.

On the Indian side, these stable but in no way immutable relations reflect imperatives of national interest which the leaders of that country have never ceased reiterating since 1947: India is neither pro-American nor pro-Soviet, it is above all pro-Indian. But this nationalism is not a mere ideological abstraction. It relates to internal and external considerations that need to be analysed in detail. Thus, the nature of the Indian state, the mode of economic development chosen by its leaders, the remarkable stability of the Congress Party or the weakness of the communist movement are all factors which determine, in varying degrees, the nature and scale of Soviet–Indian relations. At the same time, externally, China's policy since the 1950s and the US–Pakistan alliance go a long way to explain the development of relations between the two countries.

The internal determinants of the Indo-Soviet 'alliance'

The mode of development chosen by the Indian leaders following independence explains much of the initial interest of India for the USSR. What happened was that after a few years of transition (1947–51), during which it was busy establishing the bases of its new state, India gradually defined a development policy giving the public sector, heavy industry and planning a strategic role. This choice, expressed in the early years of independence by the two resolutions on industrial policy of 1948 and 1956, the first two Five-Year Plans, and the adoption by the Congress Party in 1955 of a 'socialist pattern of society', resulted, in turn, from the decisive influence exercised by social actors and principally the national bourgeoisie and the urban middle classes.

At independence, the Indian bourgeoisie had already taken on the features of a big bourgeoisie. As many official reports published subsequently testify,[1] a small number of families held an overwhelming share of the industrial, financial and commercial capital of India. These 'big families', which headed 'big industrial monopolies', to repeat the terms used by the 1965 Monopolies Inquiry Commission,[2] were the Tatas, Birlas, Dalmias, Jaïns, Goenkas, etc.

They exercise a preponderant influence in a country where the overwhelming majority of the population lives on the land and where different modes and relations of production are sometimes inextricably mixed up together. Because Indian capitalism had freed itself of British control before 1947, it could even be maintained that political independence simply endorsed an economic independence that had already been acquired.[3] And from that point of view, India's situation was quite different from that of Algeria. These big business circles, closely associated with the nationalist movement and the Congress Party,[4] quite naturally came to see the economic development of India in terms of the interests of their own group. But, thanks to an acute awareness of realities and their political maturity, they carefully assessed the weight of their influence. They knew that their economic power enabled them to contemplate for their country an economic development independent of foreign capital. In this respect, the letter addressed in 1947 by a group of industrialists to the Deputy Prime Minister Vallabhbhai Patel is indicative. He was asked to ensure that foreign ownership never exceed 30% of capital invested, and that even in exceptional circumstances control should remain in Indian hands.[5] But, at the same time, these national industrialists assessed the structural weaknesses of the Indian economy: excess of finance capital, weakness of the industrial infrastructure, and limited development of basic industrial sectors, such as steel or metallurgy.[6] In 1944, with these goals, but also these constraints in mind, the Tata group submitted to the authorities a memorandum, known as the Bombay Plan, envisaging the development of the public sector, in the area of infrastructure and heavy industry, in order to make up for the weaknesses of the big groups. Of course, the promoters of this project hoped that once the state investment had been recouped the public assets would be sold back to the private sector. But the main point is to see that the Indian bourgeoisie contemplated the satisfaction of its own interests through the development of a planned and partly nationalized economy.

This economic nationalism combined with the older but still vibrant political nationalism helps us to understand the cardinal principle of Indian foreign policy: national independence. Even though the Indian bourgeoisie is ideologically inclined to look to the West, and notably the United States, it must take account of the refusal of the West to open its markets to it or the West's fear of seeing Indian products competing with its own products. These divergences of interest, doubtless aggravated by the Cold War context, led Nehru to bitter and disillusioned reactions at the time of his first visit abroad to New York in 1949.[7] Faced with this situation, and as its options became clearer, India was tempted to look towards the USSR, a country with no colonial past and interested in promoting the industrial public sector in developing countries.

This orientation given to India's external relations was favoured by the urban intelligentsia, particularly receptive to socialist-inspired ideology. Its representatives, who held major responsible positions within and outside the state apparatus (ministries, departments, planning, universities, press), contributed decisively to shaping urban public opinion. Following the war, they counterbalanced, within the state apparatus and representative institutions, notably in parliament, the influence of the conservative and sometimes very retrograde rural elites.

In order to understand the *hegemonic* role of this social group within the state apparatus, it is important to situate it in the context of the urbanization of India. Despite the existence of a very large rural population (70% of the adult population), the big Indian cities with a long history behind them weigh heavily in the choices of industrial policy. Within the population of these cities, workers and wage-earners in the non-industrial sector predominate. In Bombay, Calcutta, Madras or Delhi, the high concentration of the working class has favoured the penetration of Marxism into India through the trade unions or left-wing parties. This working class is relatively well organized and has much more influence than its size might lead one to suppose. As for non-industrial wage-earners, even though they enjoy better living conditions than those of the rest of the population they are still not sheltered from all material difficulties:

> They feel cut off from the bourgeoisie . . . The white-collar workers and minor civil servants accept State intervention in economic affairs because of their social position. They even think it desirable. They hope that the State may protect them from being exploited by big capital, speculators, moneylenders, etc.[8]

It is thus not accidental that these social strata have contributed to producing a certain type of 'progressive' or 'socialist' intellectual. As Kochanek writes, 'the most deeply committed to a socialist ideology were the urban intellectuals'.[9] If we add to that the fact that it is in these circles that the majority of newspaper readers is recruited, it will be understood how their ideas should have influenced a large proportion of decision-makers. The personality and ideas of Jawaharlal Nehru seem to be a good illustration of this phenomenon. As Suzanne Rudolph notes, Nehru:

> constructed out of the hopes for planning and the public sector the equivalent of a charismatic ideology pointing toward a modern and socialist future. The symbolic functions of that ideology . . . were immense. It focused national attention on public, collective, and national goods, and consequently played a considerable role in 'nation-building'. It made it possible to sustain political hope in a difficult era.[10]

Thus, in the intellectual milieux where communists remained in a tiny minority, the influence (even if diffuse) of Marxism became relatively strong. Thus there was no hesitation in discussing the celebrated controversy between Lenin and the Indian communist delegate M. N. Roy at the Baku Congress on the role of the national bourgeoisie in the process of national liberation.[11] In one sense, it is doubtless not wrong to think that the very weakness of the Indian communist movement as a structured political organizer was something reassuring for the government. If the Communist Party of India had been stronger in 1947, it is likely that the Indian regime would have been more reserved towards the USSR. However that may be, Nehru, imitated in this by numerous other Third World leaders, very soon established a quite clear distinction between the Indian communists and the USSR.

Combining anti-communism with a great openness towards the Soviet Union, he was already saying before 1947:

> When [hundreds of thousands] of Indians staked their all for the country's cause, the Communists were in the opposite camp, which cannot be forgotten. The common man associates the CPI with Russia and Communism. We do not want to spoil relations with Russia, with whom we are looking forward for closer relations when India becomes independent.[12]

Indo-Soviet economic cooperation

Economic cooperation between the two countries relates primarily to the development of the public sector in the key branches of the Indian economy. It concerns over 80 projects of which some 50 are already operational. According to the Soviets:

> The enterprises established in India with the aid of the USSR, today produce over 33% of the steel, extract about 42% and refine 31% of the oil, produce 11% of the electrical energy and a considerable proportion of the country's metallurgical, mining and energy equipment.[13]

The big industrial units developed with the help of the USSR are widely known in India: Bhilai and Bokharo for steel mills, Ranchi, Durgapur and Hardwar for engineering works, Korba for aluminium. These enterprises all belong to a public sector which produces and extracts 85% of the steel, 90% of the electrical energy, 70% of the oil and 96% of the gas.[14]

This cooperation, initiated in 1955 with the signing of a cooperation agreement relating to the construction of the Bhilai complex, has become closer and closer. It is, moreover, institutionalized in an 'Indo-Soviet Intergovernmental Commission for Economic, Scientific and Technical Cooperation', responsible for coordinating, applying and developing the commitments of the two countries.[15] It is all the time extending its oversight to new sectors, such as, for example, space questions.

This growth of bilateral cooperation has naturally led to a sharp increase in Indo-Soviet trade.[16] At the beginning of the 1960s, this was negligible. By the 1970s, the USSR was catching up with the USA. In 1983, the Indian official in charge of USSR–Asia trade in the Soviet ministry of external trade could write:

> India has become one of the most important commercial partners of the USSR among the developing countries, outstripping in terms of volume the trade of the USSR with various capitalist countries, in particular the United States . . . Conversely, the USSR has become India's principal trading partner and occupies the leading place in its external trade.[17]

This trade will grow even further if we are to believe the September 1982 agreement which envisages a doubling in the volume of trade between 1979 and 1986. This rapid growth in trade was accompanied by a considerable diversification of the goods imported and exported by India. In order to meet its partner's needs, the USSR is tending to deliver more and more sophisticated equipment (excavators, drilling equipment, communication equipment, etc.) in addition to the more traditional exports of oil, raw materials and manufactured goods. For its part, India is trying increasingly to include finished or semi-finished goods in its list of exports.

The scale of trade between India and the USSR inevitably arouses much debate among Indian economists. Some of them see such flows as benefiting only the USSR, described as imperialist.[18] Others, on the other hand, see these relations as being of benefit to India.[19]

In reality, and beyond its economic or technical dimension, this debate must be related to how far close relations with the USSR are acceptable to Indian public opinion. But this controversy affects only a narrow circle of readers of specialized journals. It is not a political issue capable of mobilizing the whole country. Moreover, all governments since 1947, including the conservative one headed by Morarji Desai in the 1977–80 period, have reaffirmed their attachment to cooperation with the USSR. Such constancy doubtless reflects a certain internal political consensus and fits into the perspective of strengthening national independence such as it is perceived by the ruling elite.

This complementarity of Soviet cooperation and India's needs was moreover clearly perceived by the American Ambassador J. K. Galbraith in the 1960s: 'Our past help to private-sector plants, such as Tata's, has evoked the comment, "The Americans help the Tatas and Birlas who are already rich. By contrast the Soviets or the British build plants that belong to the people."'[20]

Elsewhere, where he discusses the difficulties he encountered in Washington in securing United States financing of the Bokharo steel plant,[21] which in the end went to the USSR, J. K. Galbraith observed that Indians' suspicion of American aid arose not only from the climate of the Cold War or American support for Pakistan, but resulted from the fact that it was perceived as 'an invasion of sovereignty'.[22] Such an appreciation is all the more significant because the total amount of American financial aid to India remains much higher than that of the USSR.

The constraints of the regional environment

Some writers feel that by the end of the 19th Century, a 'friendly image of Russia'[23] already prevailed in India, forged in reaction to British colonial domination. Supposing that it existed, this feeling was undeniably amplified by the 1917 revolution. The new Soviet state's anti-colonial policy had a considerable impact on the Indian nationalist movement, despite the efforts made by British propaganda to put it about that the USSR had hegemonic designs on India. It is inconceivable, said Nehru in 1929, 'that Russia, in her present condition at least, and for a long time, will threaten India'.[24] The future prime minister also felt that Russia and India should get along well together and that 'there was no reason for India to inherit the long Anglo-Russian rivalry'.[25] For his part, Gandhi, whose ideology scarcely predisposed him to become a fervent admirer of the October revolution, declared in 1921 'that he had never believed in the Bolshevik threat'.[26]

This Indian perception of the USSR did not alter following independence, even though the Soviet press or some high officials felt obliged to describe the Nehru government as a 'reactionary regime subject to Anglo-American imperialist influence'. In fact Nehru, who felt that he had the means to carry out his policy,[27] envisaged his relations with the USSR from two considerations. The first flowed from a simple observation: India was too vast, too populous and too complex a country to lend itself to annexation by a foreign power. The second reflected considerations of regional balance and notably the existence of a threefold American–Chinese–Pakistani constraint.

Relatively rapidly, India became convinced that the West in general and the Americans in particular were adopting a hostile attitude towards it in its conflict with Pakistan over Kashmir. But, while the first armed Indo-Pakistani conflict of 1947–49 flowed directly from the colonial heritage and the inability of the two new independent states to settle their dispute through negotiation, the second (1965), on the other hand, went beyond the limits of a mere bilateral dispute and included a new element: the American political commitment in South Asia alongside Pakistan.[28]

In order to properly understand the Indian attitude towards the United States, it must be observed that the tightening of ties between America and Pakistan (assistance and defence treaty of 1954, integration of Pakistan into SEATO in 1954 and CENTO in 1955) occurred just when Indo-Pakistan relations were showing signs of détente and when negotiations were going on between the two countries at the highest level (Nehru's visit to Karachi in 1953). As J. D. Das Gupta notes, 'In August 1953, an agreement with Pakistan with regard to Kashmir was almost in sight, in August 1954 it had disappeared completely'.[29] In fact, it is possible that Pakistan, heavily armed by the United States, felt that it enjoyed sufficient outside support to be able to launch a war against India:

> The most decisive factor undermining the potential agreement on Kashmir was American aid to Pakistan . . . [It] enabled Pakistan to carry out military operations against India . . . First, Pakistan's membership in alliances sponsored by the United States worried India and exacerbated already strained Indo-Pakistan relations. Second, by improving the military capacities of Pakistan (and, to a lesser degree, of India) the United States encouraged the arms race in South Asia. Third, by belonging to security alliances sponsored by the Americans, Pakistan was led to believe that the United States and the other partners in the alliance would support it in its disagreements with India.[30]

Thus, India, which had sought to have the best possible relations with the West, decided that American policy was opposed to its own conception of non-alignment as well as threatening its security by virtue of the Washington–Karachi alliance. This perception, which coincided with a softening of the USSR's foreign policy following Stalin's death,[31] contributed to the development of Indo-Soviet cooperation. In 1955, Khruschev travelled to New Delhi. And ten years later, the USSR, whose influence in South Asia was growing, welcomed the Indian and Pakistani belligerents in Tashkent.

While the Soviet–Indian rapprochement was helped by the regional behaviour of the United States, it was also facilitated by China's policy. Contrary to the opinion of his Deputy Prime Minister Patel,[32] Nehru, after consulting with the

Commonwealth, had no hesitation in quickly recognizing People's China, and giving way on Tibet. Subsequently, he worked actively for China's full entry on to the world diplomatic stage (notably at Bandung in 1955). But, for reasons probably in part to do with its conflict with the USSR, Beijing did not hesitate to resort to force against India in 1962. This conflict, which saw the defeat of Indian troops, altered the balance of forces in the region. As a logical consequence of the Sino-Indian confrontation, the rapprochement between China and Pakistan got underway in 1963, with a border agreement concluded between the two countries relating to a part of Kashmir claimed by India. At the time, all the implications of the 1962 conflict could not be foreseen. Today, with the perspective of time, it can be seen that it bore within it the seed of the Sino-American rapprochement. For the fact is, that the Sino-Indian conflict, which appears closely linked to the deterioration in Sino-Soviet relations, led to two opposed systems of undeclared alliances: the Washington–Karachi–Beijing axis on the one hand, the Moscow–New Delhi axis on the other. Well before the beginning of the Vietnam war, and its spread to the rest of South-East Asia, the Indian subcontinent thus appears as the first region in the world where one could observe the effects of the triangular play among the Soviet Union, the United States and China which has so profoundly marked international relations since the late 1960s. India found itself, partly despite itself, placed at the centre of this source of tensions. It very soon realized that the major European countries, most of which simply fell into step behind American policy, could be of no help to it. And the Bangladesh conflict in 1971 could only confirm it in that opinion.

In fact, for the first time in the history of the region, the American–Chinese–Pakistani entente was seen in the delivery of weapons to Pakistan, the tension on the Indian border and the despatch of an American aircraft carrier into the Bay of Bengal. In order to avoid an excessive polarization of the issues in the region, India unsuccessfully attempted an opening towards the European states, and France in particular. It was in this regional context that in August 1971 the Soviet-Indian treaty of friendship and cooperation was signed. The deterrent character of this agreement is clearly stressed in article 9:

> In case either of the parties is attacked or threatened with attack, the high contracting parties shall immediately start mutual consultations with a view to eliminating the threat and taking appropriate effective measures to ensure peace and security for their countries.[33]

This treaty has so far undeniably proved to be very effective. The scope of Soviet deterrence stands in singular contrast to America's refusal to intervene militarily alongside Pakistan, both in 1965 and 1971. The 1971 treaty appeared to India as one of the guarantees of its national security. Even the Desai government which, in its first statement on foreign affairs, talked of embarking the country on the path of 'true non-alignment' (meaning tilting India's policy to the West), took good care not to mention the possibility of any abrogation of the Soviet–Indian treaty. As long as the relation of forces in the region has not been markedly modified, it is clear that this agreement will continue to serve as the basis for the development of Indo-Soviet relations.

The future of Indo-Soviet relations

We have endeavoured to show that domestic and regional considerations have historically come together to give Indo-Soviet relations such a stable character. But, while having a stable character, these relations are still liable to evolve under the impact of changes affecting not only Indian society but also the geopolitical environment of the country.

The Indian big bourgeoisie, whose interest in the development of economic cooperation with the USSR we have stressed, today has new things to worry about. Some economists[34] feel that it has to take into account the growing contradiction between, on the one hand, the continued existence of considerable mass poverty and, on the other, hitherto unrivalled potentials for economic, cultural and technological development (India is among the top 12 industrial powers in the world). They argue that the smallness of the national market acts as a brake on such potentials, thus pushing Indian industrialists to seek outlets beyond India's borders. By gradually penetrating the markets of Africa, the Persian Gulf and the Middle East, India, which counts among the most advanced of the developing countries, is coming into competition with Western groups. But, at the same time, it may seek to find ways of associating its capital with theirs. It may also decide to open up its domestic market to some categories of foreign goods for which there is no economy of scale in India. The liberalization of the Indian investment code since 1976 is particularly significant in this respect. It coincides with a growing and indisputable integration of India into a capitalist system whose sometimes harsh rules it has to accept (see the conditions attached to the IMF loan to New Delhi in 1981).

These new conditions are leading India to modify its perception of international reality, even if the changes made take the form of discreet changes of emphasis rather than real shifts (Morarji Desai's policy between 1977 and 1980; Indira Gandhi's visit to the United States preceding her visit to the Soviet Union after her return to power).

The shift in the interests of the Indian big bourgeoisie appears to be closely connected with the profound changes in the Indian social landscape over the last 30 years. The urban intelligentsia, whose decisive political influence we have mentioned, has perhaps lost its hegemonic character. Social strata that did not exist in 1947 have appeared since then: a wealthy peasantry reinvesting on its lands according to a capitalist mode of exploitation, a small and middle industrial bourgeoisie. As a result, notably, of various agrarian reforms and nationalization of the banks, India has seen the development of different fractions of its bourgeoisie.[35] This new reality has been accompanied by the emergence of new rural and urban political elites whose political horizon is usually limited to the borders of the states, and whose spontaneous ideology goes against any socialist conception of development. The tailing off of the Congress's economic programme, reduced caricaturally during the Emergency to the five points of Sanjay Gandhi's Congress Youth, is a reflection of this evolution. Among the state ruling elites 'socialism' remains a vague term, one that is less and less structured, more and more challenged and in any event incapable of channelling the energies of these new rising classes.

In these circumstances, one can understand both the inability of the Congress Party to remain the backbone of the Indian political system, the current upsurges of regional feelings and the revitalization of the Indian communist movement undermined by the 1964 split. Since the end of the emergency, the CPI (Communist Party of India) and the CPI(M) have been coordinating their efforts more and more. They slightly improved their electoral tally at the 1980 elections faced with a divided Janata coalition.

Could the open political hostility of the two communist parties to the Indian government influence the evolution of Indo-Soviet diplomatic relations? This question has been posed since the Congress Party decided, in May 1981, to form a new pro-government Indo-Soviet friendship association to counter the influence exercised by the CPI over the previous association and to launch an all-out attack, according to some, 'dislodging pro-CPI intellectuals from strategic positions in India's educational-cultural establishment'.[36] It even seems that New Delhi would like to see Moscow put pressure on the CPI to make it moderate its hostility to government policy.

In addition to the change in India's economic and social context, and the internal political relations of force, there is the evolution of international constraints. Because in 30 years it has become an industrial and nuclear power, India aspires to play a regional role reflecting that new power. In order to assert its presence, it seeks to attenuate the effects of East–West rivalry in the Indian subcontinent and to revive the idea of non-alignment. Through advocacy of the notion 'Indian Ocean: zone of peace', India, with the support of most of the riparian states, is seeking implicitly to establish a *pax indiana* in the region. Furthermore, the weakening of tensions in the region would enable India to reduce its military expenditure so as to devote itself more to the tasks of its development.

It is in this global framework that it is possible to understand India's interest in normalizing its relations with its three principal neighbours (China, Pakistan and Bangladesh), without undermining its security. This effort was begun in the mid-1970s, pursued by Morarji Desai between 1977 and 1980, and taken up again by Mrs Gandhi's government. The dialogue with Beijing launched in 1976 is continuing. Negotiations with Pakistan are going on in circumstances which might eventually make it possible to go beyond the 1972 Simla normalization agreement. Finally, with Bangladesh, New Delhi has opened negotiations on the settlement of the issue of the sharing of the Ganges waters and the Faraka dam.

In this strategy of peace-seeking, any action by powers outside the region is looked at askance by India. This is the case with American military support for Pakistan, but also with the Soviet involvement in Afghanistan. India, which fears an increase in East–West tension in the region and which wants at all costs to prevent the development of a running sore on its borders, backs any diplomatic effort likely to lead to a withdrawal of Soviet troops and result in a political settlement of the conflict.

India's aspiration to play a growing autonomous role in the region and to stand more apart from the great powers, including the USSR, can only take concrete shape if its two regional rivals (China and Pakistan) are disposed to act to the same end. But, in current conditions, the American military support for Pakistan and the domestic problems of the Zia-ul-Haq regime prevent that country becoming what India would like it to become: a buffer state between India and the USSR, anxious to negotiate with India. As for Chinese policy, India feels that it is as yet too ill-defined to embark on a new path.

For all these reasons, and saving unforeseeable domestic upheavals, India's Soviet policy is most likely to remain constant, even if the perception of the USSR in India is tending gradually to change.

Notes

1. See R. K. Hazari, *The Structure of the Private Corporate Sector. A study of concentration, ownership and control*, Bombay, Asia Publishing House, 1966; *Report of the Monopolies Inquiry Commission*, New Delhi, Government of India Press, 1965, vols. 1 and 2; *Report of the Committee on Distribution of Income and Levels of Living*, Part 1, New Delhi, Government of India Press, February 1964.

2. Idem.

3. This does not of course mean that foreign and particularly British capital was negligible at independence. See M. Kidron, *Foreign Investment in India*, London, Oxford University Press, 1965.

4. See the memoirs of the leader of the Birla group, G. D. Birla, *In the Shadow of the Mahatma. A personal memoir*, Bombay, Orient Longman, 1953.

5. Proposal made by a 'prominent industrialist' to V. Patel. It is contained in an appendix to the letter from V. Patel to C. Rajagopalachari, dated 10 February 1947, in D. Das (ed.), *Sardar Patel's Correspondence 1945–1950*, Ahmedebad, Navajivan Publishing House, vol. 4, pp. 91–3.

6. See C. Bettelheim, *L'Inde indépendante*, Paris, Armand Colin, 1962 (Eng. tr. W. A. Caswell, *India Independent*, London, Macgibbon and Kee, 1968), and A. I. Levkosky, *Capitalism in India: Basic Trends in its Development*, Moscow, People's Publishing House, 1972.

7. See J. Nehru, *Visit to America*, New York, John Day, 1950.

8. C. Bettelheim, *India Independent*, op. cit., p. 94.

9. S. A. Kochanek, *Business and Politics in India*, Berkeley, University of California Press, 1974, p. 29.

10. S. H. Rudolph, 'The writ from Delhi', *Asian Survey*, vol. 11, 10, October 1971, p. 967.

11. Practically every book mentions this controversy. See D. Kaushik, *Soviet Relations with India and Pakistan*, Delhi, Vikas Publishers, 1970; B. Chatterjee, *Indo-Soviet Friendship. An analytical study*, New Delhi, Chand and Co., 1974; A. Stein, *India and the Soviet Union. The Nehru era*, Chicago, University of Chicago Press, 1969.

12. Quoted in A. Stein, *India and the Soviet Union*, op. cit., p. 22.

13. M. Kisselev and O. Drozdov, 'URSS–Inde: commerce et coopération', *Commerce Extérieur*, 8, 1982, p. 9.

14. See B. Tchekhonine, 'URSS–Inde: dans la voie de l'amitié et de la coopération. Vers le 35e anniversaire de l'établissement de relations diplomatiques', *La Vie Internationale*, 5, 1982, pp. 15–23 and A. Ladojski, 'URSS–Inde: vers une

consolidation de la paix', *La Vie Internationale*, 12, 1982, pp. 87–90.

15. *Pravda*, 27 September 1982, quoted in *Nouvelles de Moscou* (supplement to no. 40, October 1982, text of the joint Indo-Soviet statement, 21 September 1982).

16. See *India 1981. A reference annual*, Research and Reference Division, Ministry of Information and Broadcasting, Government of India, pp. 339–40.

17. M. Kisselev and O. Drozdov, 'URSS–Inde: commerce et coopération', op. cit., p. 9.

18. See S. K. Mehotra and P. Clawson, 'Soviet economic relations with India and other Third World countries', *Economic and Political Weekly* (Bombay), vol. 14, 30–32, 1979, pp. 1367–92.

19. See M. Sebastian, 'Does India buy dear from and sell cheap to the Soviet Union', *Economic and Political Weekly*, vol. 8, 48, 1973, pp. 2141–50.

20. J. K. Galbraith, *Journal d'un ambassadeur. Compte rendu personnel des années Kennedy*, Paris, Denoël, 1970, p. 203 (Eng. orig. *Ambassador's Journal. A personal account of the Kennedy years*, London, Hamish Hamilton, 1979, p. 215).

21. Ibid., pp. 474 and 484.

22. Ibid., p. 120.

23. B. Chatterjee, *Indo-Soviet Friendship*, op. cit., p. 13.

24. Quoted in A. Stein, *India and the Soviet Union*, op. cit., p. 26.

25. Quoted in B. Chatterjee, op. cit., p. 27.

26. Quoted in ibid., p. 24.

27. Nehru's reactions to Soviet propaganda at the time are in this respect particularly revealing; see *Indian Express*, 29 January 1966.

28. See M. J. Zins, 'Les causes des guerres indo-pakistanaises de 1947–1948, de 1965 et de 1971' (Paper presented to the colloquium at the Institut de Politique Internationale et Européenne, Nanterre, 1980), Paris, CEIAS, Maison des Sciences de l'Homme, 1980.

29. J. B. Das Gupta, *Indo-Pakistan Relations (1947–1955)*, Amsterdam, Djambatan, 1958, p. 238.

30. L. D. Hayes, 'The impact of the U.S. policy on the Kashmir conflict', *International Studies*, 2, 1971, p. 57.

31. See P. Devillers, *Guerre ou Paix. Une interprétation de la politique extérieure soviétique depuis 1944*, Paris, Balland, 1979.

32. Letter from V. Patel to J. Nehru, dated 6 December 1949 and letter from J. Nehru to V. Patel dated 6 December 1949, quoted in *Sardar Patel's Correspondence*, op. cit., vol. 8, pp. 86–8.

33. Treaty of peace, friendship and cooperation of 9 August 1971, *Izvestia*, 10 August 1971, quoted in *Problèmes politiques et sociaux*, La Documentation Française (III), 1972, p. 24 (Eng. text in *USSR and the Third World*, 15 August 1971, pp. 353–5).

34. N. Bannerjee and A. Bagchi (eds.), *Change and Choice in Indian Industry*, Calcutta, K. P. Bagchi, 1981.

35. See G. K. Shirokov, *Industrialisation of India*, Moscow, Progress Publishers, 1973.

36. B. Sen Gupta, 'The communist factor', *Seminar*, 265, September 1981, pp. 26–30.

7 The USSR's Image in Latin America

Antonio-Carlos Peixoto

The official diplomatic history of the USSR, in its latest version, devotes only three pages out of a total of 100 to Latin America.[1] Taken alone, this single figure reveals the slight place occupied by the sub-continent in the global strategy of the USSR. But this marginal position can, nevertheless, only be understood by reference to characteristics peculiar to the image of the USSR in Latin America.

Geographical distance and the weakness of historical relations go a long way to explain the weakness of their links. Tsarist Russia, a European power and secondarily an Asian one, took little interest in this region of the world.[2] It played no role in the formation of the states constituting Latin America, nor in their subsequent development all through the 19th century. Latin America rapidly found its place in the international division of labour. Placed in the orbit of Anglo-Saxon capitalism, it restricted its relations with the Russian empire to the diplomatic framework. And when the October revolution erupted, all the Latin American countries represented in St Petersburg put an end to their relations with the new Soviet republic. Only Mexico and Uruguay, which later recognized the new Soviet regime, maintained lasting relations with it until 1945.[3] The discontinuity in diplomatic relations and the absence of historical relations combined with the weakness of any commercial, cultural and migratory links. Compared with Italian, Spanish or German immigration, Russian immigration into Latin America was always very small. 'White Russians', present above all in Argentina and southern Brazil, represented only a tiny percentage of the total number of immigrants who had chosen these two countries.

In order to break its diplomatic isolation in this region of the world, the USSR explored the paths of commercial cooperation. In 1925, a first delegation representing Amtorg (the state agency for trade with America) was sent to Buenos Aires. The following year, an Argentine cargo ship inaugurated the first shipping link between the USSR and Latin America by unloading a cargo of leather and *quebracho* at Odessa.

In 1927, Amtorg opened a first commercial representation in Buenos Aires, then a second in Rio Grande in Brazil shortly afterwards. Under the second Yrigoyen government, Buenos Aires even inaugurated technical cooperation with the USSR for the exploitation of oil. But the political change in Argentina in 1930 put a halt to its development. The Soviets transferred the seat of Amtorg from Buenos Aires to Montevideo in 1931; and when four years later, diplomatic relations between the

USSR and Uruguay were broken, commercial relations fell off to such a point as to become largely symbolic.

It was not until the end of the Second World War and the accession of the USSR to the rank of victorious great power alongside the allies, that there was a rapprochement between Moscow and the various Latin American capitals. Diplomatic relations with Brazil and Argentina were restored in 1945 and 1946 respectively. The circumstances in which this evolution occurred are interesting and worth telling. In a memorandum dating from 1944, the Itamaraty (Brazilian ministry of foreign affairs) authorized the heads of Brazilian diplomatic missions to maintain their personal contacts with Soviet representatives.[4] In February 1944, the Brazilian Foreign Minister, Oswaldo Aranha, declared himself in favour of a resumption of diplomatic relations with the USSR. At the same time, the Mexican Minister of Foreign Affairs offered the Brazilian ambassador his good offices to hasten such a rapprochement. At the end of 1944, the Itamaraty indirectly justified this possibility:

> The development of this political ideology [communism] is a vanguard phenomenon which does not depend for its propaganda on the isolation of Russia. The evil effects of communist propaganda must be fought by the police where they take the form of crimes against state security, and through teaching, persuasion and counter-propaganda when they are limited to the doctrinal level alone.[5]

Paradoxically, moreover, the last obstacles to the normalization of Soviet–Brazilian relations were lifted by the United States. On his return from the Yalta conference, the American Secretary of State, Edward Stettinius, stopped over in Rio in February 1945 to persuade Brazil to normalize its relations with Moscow, furthermore, the negotiations which ended in the re-establishment of diplomatic relations between the two countries took place in Washington in April 1945.[6]

The Soviet–Argentine rapprochement occurred in rather different circumstances. In fact, while in the case of Brazil normalization came in agreement with Washington – in spite of American hostility to the Vargas government – in the case of Argentina it was a frontal disagreement with the United States that led to the resumption of diplomatic relations with Moscow. The American–Argentine dispute in the years 1944–46 was a major one, and it does not seem useful to mention here in detail the numerous incidents that marked the American Ambassador S. Braden's stay in Buenos Aires.[7] It seems interesting, however, to note that despite the deterioration in American–Argentine relations, the Soviet Union continued to express serious reservations about Argentina. At the Yalta conference, Stalin had pressed for sanctions against Argentina which he accused of not having cooperated with the allies. At the San Francisco conference, Molotov again raised the question by skilfully proposing to tie the admission of Argentina to that of Byelorussia, the Ukraine and the Polish Lublin government.[8] But this policy of obstruction was short-lived. The election of Peron to the Argentine presidency in February 1946 provoked an exacerbation of the tension between the United States and Argentina:

> As a result of the policy that the United States has pursued towards Argentina during the preceding two and a half years, this country had received at the hands

of the Argentine people the worst diplomatic defeat it ever sustained in the Western Hemisphere and had suffered a loss of influence and of prestige in South America that will not be forgotten for many years to come.[9]

The USSR, whose relations with the United States were beginning to become strained, could no longer ignore the advantages of a rapprochement with Buenos Aires, which for its part sought to affirm its independence of Washington.

The difference of context in which the normalization of relations between Brazil and Argentina and the Soviet Union took place, helps us to understand why Brazil again broke off relations at the beginning of the Cold War while Argentina endeavoured to maintain them.[10] The Brazilian diplomatic alignment on Washington was probably the reason for this new break. But it is equally likely that the attitude of the PCB (Brazilian Communist Party) facilitated the choice by the Brazilian authorities. In fact, the arrival of the Soviet Ambassador in Rio de Janeiro in 1946 had been greeted with large welcoming demonstrations organized by the PCB. Furthermore, a series of diplomatic incidents hastened this breach, of which the first, a very minor affair, had to do with the misfortunes of a Brazilian diplomat caught up in a night brawl in Moscow. This affair, which was really a very ordinary one of no great importance, would have had no lasting effects if it had not been blown up in the Brazilian press.[11] More serious was the recall of the Soviet Ambassador in May 1947 following the Brazilian government's banning of the PCB. This gesture was interpreted in Rio at the time as an act of interference in the domestic affairs of Brazil. But it was the publication of an article in the Soviet press deemed to be insulting to the head of state and armed forces of Brazil that precipitated the break of diplomatic relations.[12]

While Brazil used these incidents as a pretext for a break that was going to happen anyway, the USSR for its part made no effort to prevent it. Its attitude, too, was very probably dictated by the imperatives of the Cold War. But this conjunctural factor needs to be linked to two major constraints that the USSR met with in Latin America: the first flows from the weight of the political influence of the United States in the region. The second can be deduced from the absence of any specific regional problematic in Latin America that might facilitate an increase in Soviet influence. In Africa and Asia, decolonization allowed the USSR to ally with the liberation movements and subsequently establish close relations with some of the new states. In the Middle East, the Palestinian question also offered it a channel to increase its influence. In Latin America, it is the question of development that has been at the centre of the regional problematic since the late 1950s. For some years, this same question seems in some countries to have become closely linked to the problem of political democracy. But, faced with such issues, the Soviet contribution can only be limited. The Soviet message on underdevelopment seems ambiguous. Soviet Marxism–Leninism considers imperialism, and more particularly North American imperialism, as the chief obstacle to the material progress of developing countries. Participating in the struggle against underdevelopment alongside governments presented and described as favourable to imperialism would amount to strengthening such regimes and consequently legitimizing a capitalist-type economic model. In addition, the Soviet Union seems to experience real difficulties in taking part individually or collectively in a true policy of financing development.

Remaining outside the large financial flows towards Latin America from the developed countries and specialized institutions, the USSR participates only modestly in the external economic activity of Latin American countries.[13] The USSR is badly equipped to meet the economic expectations of the countries of Latin America and it is equally ill-equipped to understand the democratic challenge that these countries are attempting to take up. At this level, the obstacle is very certainly ideological in nature. But, it also has to do with the fact that, unlike the United States, the Soviet Union has no network of local influence on which it can count. In such circumstances, its goals are limited to strengthening its influence when the occasion arises, weakening the hegemonic position of the United States, and defending the Cuban regime. This prudent, usually wait-and-see policy, naturally leads it to move into any space opened up by conflicts born of tensions between the United States and a Latin American state. But the limits to the growth of its political influence are, in such circumstances, rarely linked to the nature of the existing regimes.

At first, Moscow endeavoured to identify the potential sources of conflict between these regimes and the United States and to propose, where relevant, alternative solutions, in so far as its means allow. Thus, and without intervening directly in a conflict, the USSR helps to strengthen the Latin American states' bargaining position and weaken the American one.

This strategy nevertheless runs up against numerous obstacles, not all of which are to be explained by the Soviet fear of avoiding a confrontation with the United States. Economically, the USSR has only a low capacity to finance the supply of technological goods. But, if it seeks to acquire a significant level of influence in a Latin American country, it will have to meet two essential conditions: 1) That the Latin American government in question is disposed to maintain or increase tension with Washington and hence take the risk of a total rupture; and 2) that this government be fully aware of the fact that Soviet material aid will be largely inadequate.

While the evolution of the Castro regime in Cuba has largely conformed to this pattern, it was quite different with the Popular Unity regime in Chile. Well before the *coup d'état* which overthrew President Allende, Chile's economic situation had become alarming. The rate of inflation was over 100% while industrial production was falling markedly. The fall in the price of copper, combined with the difficulties encountered trying to obtain short-term loans from US banks, made it very difficult to acquire the necessary foreign exchange for the import of food. But, not only was Salvador Allende slow in turning to the Soviet Union, but in addition, the result of his visit to Moscow in December 1972 was, to say the least, disappointing. He succeeded in obtaining only a $30 million credit from the Soviets intended for the import of foodstuffs and a roll-over of $20 million for short-term loans previously granted.

In fact, most of the external financial credit granted to Chile to import cereals and meat came from countries such as Argentina, Australia and Canada. In real terms, Chilean debt to all communist countries increased only very slightly – from $19 million to $40 million between 1970 and 1973 – while at the same time, loans from other Latin American countries (except Cuba) and Spain increased from $9 million to $150 million.[14] These figures alone are enough to demonstrate the Soviet Union's unwillingness to become involved in a situation comparable to that of Cuba in the early 1960s.

This Soviet prudence in Chile was repeated in Peru under President Alvarado between 1968 and 1975. Mainly, Moscow was trying to move into a space opened up by the conflict between Peru and the United States. In this case as in others, it first tried to assess the scale of the dispute between Washington and Lima. Then, it sought ways and means of cooperating with a regime that talked of alleviating 'imperialist control'. The capitalist content of the Peruvian revolution and the military nature of the Lima regime did not put obstacles in the way of Soviet policy to the extent that this policy assumed that any nationalist and hence anti-imperialist stance was bound to conflict with North American interests. The Soviet presence then appears as a channel for the expression of the anti-imperialist potential of the regime and, at the same time, as a source of increasing tension with the United States.

In its perception and analysis of the conflicts between the Latin American states and the United States, Soviet diplomacy takes into consideration the various motivations of local actors. It probably makes a distinction between a government whose political project and diplomatic orientations involve a confrontation with Washington, and another that has no hesitation in getting into a trial of strength with the United States but remains staunchly anti-communist. But this capacity to distinguish is not necessarily accompanied by differentiated diplomatic behaviour. Whether it is 'progressive' or 'pro-imperialist', a Latin American government will be dealt with only in terms of its contradictions with the United States and, secondarily, of the means that are available to the USSR to respond to its economic expectations.

Thus, the profile of Soviet diplomacy in Latin America seems resolutely 'defensive'. Its shift to a more 'offensive' level involves overcoming a number of awkward constraints.

Among these constraints, the dominant political culture in Latin America negatively affects the process of forming the USSR's image in the region.[15] This culture results both from the historical nature of social relations and the reference values of Latin American elites (ideologies, representations of the external world). Social relations in Latin America are shot through with persistent forms of patrimonialist domination which, as it breaks down, leads to mass, rather than class, situations. The state's hold on civil society has engendered numerous modes of representation, whether formal (parties, trade unions) or informal (role of influence, clientelism, direct representation of interest groups within the state), that are often more relevant than the traditional frameworks of political representation. To be effective, political domination thus involves control of the state apparatus, since mere use of the instances of civil society appears insufficient to counter action by the state or express certain demands. In local Latin American political life, charisma sometimes plays a central role. The alliances and coalitions of individual or collective actors are determined in relation to the play of power, without it always being possible to identify the social issues that underlie them. National populism illustrates this reality perfectly: the projects for all-embracing change that it advocates are disseminated by coalitions endowed with vague political programmes which have something for all social actors.

In these systems where social relations are disarticulated and the political culture fragmented, Marxism experiences tremendous difficulties in making itself into a dominant ideological pole capable of modifying the organization of the political. Its totalizing character clashes with traditional political practices. It is also at odds with the political strategies that endeavour to clarify social and political issues without necessarily referring to the concept of social class. In such conditions, Marxism becomes either the refuge of a few intellectual movements or the ideological referent of groups organized in national liberation fronts within which the presence of communist parties is very slight, or even non-existent. Moreover, in many cases, the communist parties have been suspicious of these movements with their 'adventurist' political line. Additionally it should be pointed out that the now commonplace dissociation between Marxism and Soviet power has long been the practice in Latin America. Large segments of the Latin American Left judge the Soviet Union by its political practices rather than in relation to its claimed fidelity to Marxism. The attachment of the Latin American Left to the Cuban revolution does not usually involve a doctrinal fidelity to the USSR.

The dissemination of a favourable image of the USSR, limited among the Latin American Left, is even more so among the traditional elites whether conservative or liberal, strongly influenced by Catholicism. The so-called modern elites, born of industrialization and strongly impregnated by the notion of economic profitability, do not seem to be receptive to the attractions of the Soviet model.

In these conditions, the propaganda of the communist parties in favour of the USSR can have only limited effects. Moreover, when it is not the political culture that hinders the dissemination of a positive image of the USSR, it is generally the apparatuses of official repression that take charge of countering the effects of such propaganda. That is why the communist parties in the last analysis are more concerned with delivering an anti-American message rather than a truly pro-Soviet one.

Given all these features, it can be said of the USSR's image in Latin America that it is at once subjective, of low intensity and very largely negative. It has also remained particularly stable since the Cuban revolution, even if the current development of crises in Central America is likely to affect this last parameter.

The USSR seen by Argentina and Brazil

Unlike the other countries of Latin America, Argentina and Brazil have gone beyond the stage of economic underdevelopment. Without concerning ourselves here with the different meanings of the concept of underdevelopment, we simply note that the international agencies specialized in these problems, such as the World Bank, classify these two states in the – admittedly very vague – category of NICs (Newly Industrializing Countries). The fact is that these two countries have solid industrial structures enabling them to produce a large range of industrial goods, including in some cases high technology products. Furthermore, and unlike such countries as Singapore, Taiwan or Hong Kong, which work solely to export, Brazil and Argentina have large domestic markets. Their external economic relations thus seek for the most part on the one hand to acquire high technology goods and capital resources and on the other to seek outlets for their surplus industrial and agricultural output.

For a number of structural reasons, the USSR appears incapable of becoming part of the network of external economic relations of these two states. Like Argentina and Brazil, the USSR is an importer of high technology goods; and, while it has quite a wide range of products that might interest its Latin American partners (turbines, dam construction technology), it has to compete with sharp competition from the Western capitalist countries. At the level of imports, the absorption capacities of the Soviet market for Argentine or Brazilian goods seem to be rather small, limited, in fact, to cereals in the case of Argentina and tropical agricultural produce in that of Brazil. That is why outside exceptional conjunctural periods, the Soviet market appears incapable of occupying a dynamic position in the external economic relations of Argentina and Brazil.

The Carter administration's decision in 1980 to order an embargo on cereal exports to the USSR showed what a role the Soviet market could play for Latin America in a particular situation. Thus, Argentina, which refused to join the American embargo, succeeded in quadrupling in a year its cereal sales to the USSR. They rose from 1,876 million tons in 1979 to 7,580 million tons the following year. In 1982, 75% of the cereals exported by Argentina were consigned to Soviet ports. Despite its spectacular character, this sizeable increase in Soviet–Argentine trade is not such as to alter the centre of gravity of the external economic relations of Argentina. In fact, the quantitative growth of Soviet-Argentine relations is unbalanced, reflecting the USSR's difficulty in penetrating the Argentine market.[16] In 1982, while Soviet imports had reached $1.4 billion, exports were barely more than the derisory figure of $21 million, which is why it is reasonable to speculate that the lifting of the American embargo by the Reagan administration will return Soviet–Argentine trade to more modest proportions.

It must, however, be seen that the existence, even if only temporary, of a large trade deficit favourable to Argentina can paradoxically become advantageous to the USSR. In fact, because of its high indebtedness and its cereal surpluses, Argentina sees in the USSR a stable market providing hard currency. It is thus naturally inclined toward good relations with the USSR, especially as, in some precise cases, the Western refusal to satisfy some of its technological needs makes it turn to the USSR as the last resort. Thus, in the nuclear sector, the USSR has become one of Argentina's main suppliers of heavy water and enriched uranium. But, by virtue of their limited character, such examples are not likely to undermine our initial hypothesis on the inability of the USSR to respond to the economic expectations of such countries as Argentina or Brazil. This permanent reality affects the intensity of the image (the limits to the development of relations with the USSR seem to be clearly established), its stability and its quality (the technocratic elites of these countries judging that the USSR does not have much to offer economically).

These structural mechanisms blocking the economic influence of the USSR are similarly manifest on the diplomatic level. Taking the case of Brazil, it will be observed that its diplomatic objectives have been remarkably stable for at least 20 years. They have undergone no notable shift, except perhaps during the Castelo Branco interlude (1964–66), when Brazil aligned itself more closely to American policy.

Like Argentina, Brazil proclaims loud and clear that it belongs to the Western world, even if some requirements of its economic or external policy lead it to identify itself with the Third World or to associate itself with some of its demands. That is why the existence of conflicts with other Western countries, and notably the United States, is interpreted in Brasilia as the natural expression of divergences with allies and not as a sign of defiance towards the West. In such conditions, the Soviet card appears to have too little credibility to be able to be used in bargaining with Washington. Moreover, such an eventuality would probably be rejected by virtually every segment of the elite influencing Brazilian external policy. Given its economic and ideological options, it is hard to see Brazil seeking a political–military guarantee in Moscow.

On this last point the case of Argentina is distinctly different. The Falklands war did not transform Buenos Aires' external alliances, but it did lead to serious tension with Washington from which the USSR naturally benefited. Thus, if the feeling of being rejected and humiliated by the West persisted, Argentina might come round to stepping up its relations with Moscow, especially as the economic basis exists for a strengthening of cooperation between the two countries. That is an eventuality which should not be overlooked, even if the evolution of Soviet–Argentine relations since the end of the Falklands war and the advent of democracy do not necessarily point in this direction.

Notes

1. B. Ponoramiov et al., *Historia de la politica exterior de la URSS*, Moscow, Progress Publishers, 1974.

2. The Russian empire had established diplomatic relations with Argentina, Brazil, Bolivia, Costa Rica, Chile, Cuba, Mexico, Panama, Peru and Uruguay.

3. Mexico recognized the new Soviet regime in 1924. Uruguay followed it two years later, but broke relations with the USSR in 1935.

4. *Rétablissement des relations diplomatiques entre le Brésil et l'Union Soviétique*, Rio, Itamaraty, 1962, roneo., p. 6. This publication of the Brazilian ministry of foreign affairs constituted the main source of information on this development.

5. Ibid., p. 32.

6. Ibid., p. 34.

7. The American Ambassador, S. Braden, favoured the opposition in Peru and this encouraged his fall.

8. See A. Conil Paz and G. E. Ferrari, *Argentina's Foreign Policy 1930–1962*, Notre Dame, University of Notre Dame Press, 1966.

9. Ibid.

10. Brazil re-established diplomatic relations with the USSR in 1961. Soviet–Argentine relations have been unbroken since 1945.

11. On the Soviet and Brazilian versions of the incident, see *Rétablissement des relations diplomatiques*, op. cit., p. 42.

12. Ibid., p. 27.

13. This reality is not peculiar to Latin America, even though it seems more obvious on the sub-continent: see on this point, R. H. Donaldson (ed.), *The Soviet Union in the Third World: Successes and Failures*, Boulder, Westview Press, 1981.

14. Ibid., p. 41.

15. We have here simply touched on the main features of Latin American political life without making any attempt to develop them systematically.

16. *Financial Times*, 28 February 1983.

Index